ALSO BY GABRIELLE REECE

Big Girl in the Middle

MY FOOT IS TOO BIG FOR THE GLASS SLIPPER

A GUIDE TO THE LESS THAN PERFECT LIFE

GABRIELLE REECE

WITH KAREN KARBO

Scribner

New York   London   Toronto   Sydney   New Delhi

SCRIBNER
A Division of Simon & Schuster, Inc.
1230 Avenue of the Americas
New York, NY 10020

First Scribner hardcover edition April 2013

SCRIBNER and design are registered trademarks of The Gale Group, Inc.,
used under license by Simon & Schuster, Inc., the publisher of this work.

For information about special discounts for bulk purchases,
please contact Simon & Schuster Special Sales at 1-866-506-1949
or business@simonandschuster.com.

The Simon & Schuster Speakers Bureau can bring authors to your
live event. For more information or to book an event contact the
Simon & Schuster Speakers Bureau at 1-866-248-3049 or visit our
website at www.simonspeakers.com.

Designed by *Kyle Kabel*

Manufactured in the United States of America

1   3   5   7   9   10   8   6   4   2

Library of Congress Control Number: 2012037903

ISBN 978-1-4516-9266-2
ISBN 978-1-4516-9270-9 (ebook)

For Reece, Brody, Bela, my friends, and my lover, Laird

If you happen to read fairy tales, you will observe that one idea runs from one end of them to the other—the idea that peace and happiness can only exist on some condition.

—G. K. Chesterton

The idea of my life as a fairy tale is itself a fairy tale.

—Grace Kelly

Live in the sunshine, swim in the sea, drink the wild air's salubrity.

—Ralph Waldo Emerson

CONTENTS

MY FOOT IS
TOO BIG FOR THE
GLASS SLIPPER

1

SO YOU'VE GOT THE GUY ON THE BIG WHITE HORSE

My happily ever after began on November 30, 1997. On that day I married my prince in the middle of the gently winding Hanalei River, on the north shore of the garden island of Kaua'i. Ever resourceful, my prince lashed together a pair of canoes and affixed a platform on top of them, then decorated it with purple orchids, tuberose, and plumeria. During the only sun break of the day, we exchanged vows.

My prince was bare-chested and wore a *pareo*, a wrap-around skirt traditional for men of the Pacific Islands. He looked even more studly than usual. I wore a white Calvin Klein bikini beneath a sheer white Donna Karan dress. I might as well just confirm what you're already thinking: I looked completely fabulous. (What you don't know, of course, is that I was a hot mess only an hour before, madly doing laundry and scrubbing the bathroom for our out-of-town visitors.)

After the ceremony, we repaired with our dozen guests, close friends all, to Hanalei Bay, where we had a champagne picnic. It was the perfect ending to the fairy-tale courtship that had begun two years ago that very day.

Naturally, four years later I filed for divorce.

My childhood was rough enough to knock the belief in happily ever after clean out of my heart. My parents split when I was too young to remember; then, when I was five, my dad died in a plane crash. I've always been one of those hard-headed chicks who believe that we're all responsible for our own happiness. Still, when I married Laird I was confident I'd found my soul mate. Who could be more perfect for me than a guy who was my height—six feet three—and was even more intense and focused than I was?

Laird and I met in 1995 while I was shooting a TV show called *The Extremists*. Like pretty much everything else these days, you can find it online. I was twenty-five and wore an oversized white T-shirt. My hair—are those *bangs*?—is whipping around in the wind. The sky behind me is angry with bruise-colored clouds.

"Today I'm hangin' with an extremist who catches some serious waves," I say. "His name is Laird Hamilton and he lives for the big swell."

I ask him whether he considers this to be a big swell day, and even though it looks as if a hurricane is about to roll in at any second, he says no. Laird looked exactly the same way he looks right this minute: tan and focused. You can see us falling in love right there on camera. Ten days later we moved in together.

We didn't even make it to our fifth anniversary before our sexy fairy tale turned into one of those unwatchable Swedish domestic dramas that makes the audience want to throw themselves off the nearest bridge. We were so simpatico in so many ways, but stupidly we'd counted on this fact to remain immutable and provide an unshakable foundation for our relationship. Our love was and is complex. We were lovers, friends, and partners. We weren't simply hot for each other, or companionable good friends, or a couple who had been together so long marriage was the obvious next step. We had it all covered; then, without knowing how it happened, we'd become two really tall near-strangers stomping around the house, fuming, slamming doors, and glaring at each other over our green smoothies.

How clueless was I about marriage, about living under the same roof with another human being with—surprise!—his own personality and his own life? Those who know my husband call him the Weatherman. I don't put a lot of stock in astrology, but he is one of the world's primo watermen and a Pisces—known for their deep sensitivity and mutable moods. It took being married to him to learn that he was more emotional than I'd ever imagined, and moody. Life with Laird: it's windy, no wait, it's raining, wait, wait, now it's sunny. It hardly mattered what put him in a mood (if you guessed it usually had to do with there being no surfable waves that day, you'd be right), because like the temperamental weather in Kaua'i where he grew up, it would all blow over in a few hours.

The problem was not the moods—that's who the guy is—but me. I took every slammed cupboard door personally. I thought, if he loved me, he'd be happy most of the time. I'm not the Weatherman, it's never windy/rainy/sunny with me. It's San Diego with me, 75 degrees all year long. I'm constant and true, but I hang on to shit. His mood, the one that would make me feel unloved, would be long gone, but I'd still be feeling the sting of it, the injustice. I'd still be experiencing his mood, long after he was out of it.

But I would never *say* anything, which became the problem that compounded the problem, a layer cake of misery. It's never one thing that tanks the economy or ruins a marriage. I didn't communicate, didn't tell him when he was being a jackass, didn't tell him how hurt my feelings were. I thought that when you love somebody you don't make a fuss. As a professional athlete, one of the first things I'd learned was to suck it up, and that's what I thought you did when the person with whom you were in a relationship was an ass. You sucked it up.

My friends would come over, and if Laird was in a mood, I would warn them to tread lightly. I would fret when the surf report was bad. My mantra was don't rock the boat. But after three years of tiptoeing around the Weatherman and his mercurial moods, I thought: *peace out, I can't do this anymore*. I was curbing my personality for his sake. I was becoming bitter and resentful. And if there's one thing that trashes a love story, it's resentment.

To make matters more challenging still, when Laird and I got together, my career was, well, bigger, grander, whatever you want to call it, than his. I was captaining a team on the professional beach volleyball circuit, scoring glossy magazine covers with the matching big feature stories, hosting *The Extremists*. I'd just signed a contract to write a book, and I was set to make my film debut. I had a sponsorship with Nike, and I was the first female athlete to have her own shoe. By all the markers by which people measure quote unquote success, I had them and Laird didn't.

This made me ridiculously uncomfortable. If there's one person on earth who truly does not give a shit about fame and worldly success, it's my husband. Don't get me wrong. The dude is bursting with ambition, but it's the ambition to have the most fun surfing the biggest, best wave for as long as he possibly can, the ambition to keep the sport of surfing exciting and relevant into the future. Even to this day, we'll be watching some news show and I'll say check out this guy, he's Prince Fabulous, he's got this, that, and the other: a great gig, an innovative idea, money for nothing, and chicks for free. Laird is unmoved. He's got a clarity about what's important, always has. He's only interested in how people are in the world, what they do, how they act. He's never swept up in the hoopla.

Still, during the few first years we were together, Neptune,

King of the Sea, spent many days and weeks traveling with me on the beach volleyball circuit. Chicago, St. Louis, Detroit, New York. You'd be amazed where you can build a beach. He did it because he loved me, and because with Laird there is no halfway. He was *in*, even when it meant being called Mr. Reece.

The whole scene was awkward. Even though I was a bigger deal celebritywise, and even though my success dominated the relationship, his personality dominated mine. This may come as a surprise to those people who may recall that I held the WBVL's record for most kills four years running, or that I was named the Offensive Player of the Year the summer before that fateful day on the north shore of Maui where I met and fell for Laird. We've never been one of those modern, hip couples where it's been clear from the first kiss that he'll be fine hanging at home supporting her career by doing the laundry and planning the meals and she'll be out in the world hammering it down and supporting the family.

By Christmas of 2000 I was done. The marriage had broken down, and I didn't feel like fixing it. Part of me had withdrawn. I thought: *Who needs this shit?* When I was young my motto was "nothing and no one is above my own survival," and after four years my marriage to Laird was threatening my sense of myself. I was downplaying my independence, my sense of humor, my competence, my celebrity (such as it was) in order to be with him. Every day I was consciously trying to make everything about me smaller to minimize the friction in our relationship.

So I filed for divorce.

For a while, Laird tried to talk me out of it, but then he let me go.

Then as now, we spent half the year in California, and half the year in Hawaii. When I called it quits Laird was in Kaua'i and I was in Malibu. He packed up every last thing of mine in the Hawaii house and stuck it in storage. You can imagine what a good time this was for him—he who plunges into one of his moods if he can't get out of the house and into the ocean by 7:30 a.m.—spending days shoving the T-shirts, panties, and notebooks of the chick he still wanted into cardboard cartons, taping them shut, lugging them out to the car.

I attempted to "move on"—one of those phrases that we all use without being a hundred percent sure what it means or how you do it—and threw myself into my work, a time-honored coping mechanism. The days were all right, but every morning I awoke with an ache in my gut. It felt as if one of those rawhide bones that dogs love to chew was sitting in my stomach.

Then, in the spring, Laird passed through California, and arrived at the house in Malibu to pick up his snowboard. One of the paradoxical things about Laird is that even though he's a great-looking guy, he's not a flirt (actually, maybe he's not a flirt because he *is* good-looking; he doesn't need to do anything to gain attention once he's entered the room).He'd completely disengaged from me. He was all business.

I saw clearly at that moment that he'd always been a generous, loving partner, and that his love had been a gift. He'd withdrawn it, and now I was just some chick who was holding on to his snowboard. It was then, after he'd fully stepped away, that I was able to look at him and see what I would be missing. For the first time I realized that he was a person with whom I had a good shot at happiness.

There are thousands of people out there with ideas about how to be happy and happily married and live the dream and own the happily ever after (which you already know I have no aptitude for, having messed up my marriage almost instantly).

A lot of them are men without children, or loners, or people who have other people to do the tedious shit that drives everyone who has to do it—and who isn't a complete Zen master—insane. Does Eckhart Tolle go to Costco every week for his family to make sure they have plenty of frozen three-berry mix for their smoothies and Pirate's Booty for healthy snacking? Does Deepak Chopra spend most of his waking hours washing towels that his family dropped on the bathroom floor and then trampled with their muddy feet? Gandhi was out there starving by himself, changing the world for the better, but let's not forget, Mrs. Gandhi was at home with the kids. What I'm saying is that it's easy to be your best self when you don't live in the world of "Clear your plate," "Stop whining and go to bed," "Did you brush your teeth?" "Honey, have you seen my clean shirt?" "Honey, what's for dinner?" "Honey, we haven't had sex in a month."

I'm not beating up on these guys. They've offered a lot of

wisdom, advice, solace, and inspiration to thousands, if not millions of people. They are not, however, married to a guy who doesn't do email.

I am.

Laird and I got back together. For another year or two, we circled each other, unsure. We were like survivors of some natural disaster, grateful to be alive, but dazed by the wreckage. The foundation was cracked, the roof had leaks, the windows were smashed out. Repairs always take longer—and cost more—than you might first imagine.

When we met, Laird was already respected in the world of surfing. As time went on, his star began to rise in the world at large. In 2004, he executive produced and starred in *Riding Giants*, and then a few years later he appeared in a big American Express campaign. He got to show the world that he wasn't just some guy who wandered around in swim trunks and flip-flops calling everyone Dude. (Which he never does, by the way.) This cultural stamp of approval helped to even out our personal playing field. I felt more comfortable because he was no longer simply Mr. Reece, trailing around behind me, carrying my gym bag from tournament to magazine shoot and home again. It wasn't as if the worldly success meant a lot to him personally, but it allowed us both to feel as if we were now on equal footing, careerwise. A friend once reminded me that small changes can result in making the big picture a whole lot better, and that's what happened to us.

As I write this, we've been married sixteen by-and-large happy years. In celebrity years, this translates to about nine million. It hasn't been perfect. The degree to which it's been imperfect would shock even those people who claim to thrive on imperfection. We had first one kid, then another. In 2007, we weathered another rough patch, and almost called it quits again. Through it all, I reminded myself of Anne Morrow Lindbergh's wisdom. At times, I've been on the verge of tattooing it up one leg and down the other. Instead, I just committed it to memory:

> *When you love someone, you do not love them all the time, in exactly the same way, from moment to moment. It is an impossibility. It is even a lie to pretend to. And yet this is exactly what most of us demand. We have so little faith in the ebb and flow of life, of love, of relationships. We leap at the flow of the tide and resist in terror its ebb. We are afraid it will never return. We insist on permanency, on duration, on continuity; when the only continuity possible, in life as in love, is in growth, in fluidity—in freedom, in the sense that the dancers are free, barely touching as they pass, but partners in the same pattern.*

Partners in the same pattern. That's a better thing to aspire to than happily ever after. In all those fairy tales, and also in a lot of Hollywood movies you wind up Netflixing, the story ends at the happily ever after. It's pure bullshit. Nothing makes you superficially more happy than the first flushes of love, but in the ever after it's all about dealing with your lover, with understanding what makes him tick, surviving his crappy moods, and working together, always, to preserve what you've got and nurture a deeper, more profound and grounded love into the future. Happily schmappily. I don't think so.

From a dramatic perspective, this also means there's nothing left to tell. The good part of the tale has already been told. If we're lucky, we're married fifty or sixty years. Do you want to sign up for that? Half a century or more of no conflict, no drama, no restlessness, no opportunity to grow and change? You don't want that, do you? Rather than happily ever after, we should aspire to game on—in part because that's the reality and in part because it's much more interesting.

2

ENTER LITTLE MERMAIDS

When Laird and I got back together in 2001 it wasn't like the movies. There was no single moment where we gazed at each other across his surfboard and all was forgiven. All of 2002 was difficult. We sidestepped each other, a little bruised and extra polite. He was distant, some part of him convinced that I would bolt at any minute. This wasn't the reason I became pregnant with our first daughter, but I was well aware that nothing says, "hey, we're in this together," like having a baby. Now and forever, it's the living, squealing physical manifestation of a commitment.

I'm whatever the opposite of subservient is, so I think it was always in the back of Laird's mind that I could up and leave at any time. Which was not incorrect. We always assume it's the guy in the relationship who's going to disappear one day, but in my experience as often as not the woman calls it quits.

I was never one of those girls who always knew she wanted to be a mom, but I did know that if and when I got pregnant, I would feel more tied to Laird. We already had one child, Bela, from Laird's first marriage, but I was thirty-three and said that if we were going to have another kid, we'd better do it soon. We'd been together for eight years by then. "Soon" was interpreted by the universe as "on the first try," and Reece Viola was born nine months later.

I'm an athlete. I stayed in good shape and ate well throughout my pregnancy. My first rude awakening of motherhood was the fact that my good health and fitness did nothing to guarantee an easy delivery. After thirteen hours of active labor I was advised by my doctor to have an epidural.

"You'll be too tired to push when the time comes," he said. After another seven hours of labor and two hours of pushing, he ordered a C-section. I felt like a failure, then perked up when I realized this excruciating difficulty was a mere preview of coming attractions. If my body—the faithful instrument I'd trained and pressed into service for years—had a mind of its own when it came to childbirth, what other surprises were lying in wait for me? I realized at that moment that the only thing I could count on was that I couldn't count on anything to be the way I'd imagined it.

PREPARE TO BE AMAZED

Before you've had kids, there's nothing more off-putting than having your friends with children tell you how life will never be the same. You think they've lost sight of the fact that there's a big wide world out there with people in it who are, amazingly, not them or their children. Then you have your baby and you're like the high school graduate who's flipped the tassel on his cap to the other side. Now you're the obnoxious person telling other people life will never be the same.

What we mean (because I, too, have become one of those obnoxious people) is that *you* have changed. You're you, but with the mother function switched on. You may have felt maternal toward a nephew or a kitten before this moment, but it's nothing like this. Becoming a mother is like being bitten by the spider that turns Peter Parker into Spiderman. Life will never be the same because *you* will never be the same.

My main fantasy when I was pregnant was that my baby would be born as a three-year-old. None of those swaddled, bald, little old men in the nursery for me. I wanted an insta-child born with the language skills to tell me what she wanted, potty trained, and with the teeth required to eat a burrito.

With this in mind, I'd hired a night nurse who came highly recommended. She was locally famous for helping mothers with twins and said to possess unmatched competence and efficiency. The nurse arrived the same day I came home from the hospital with Reece, and the first thing I did was pay her for two weeks of work and let her go. I didn't want anyone to come between me and my baby, a squalling, damp itsy-bitsy newborn.

I never imagined this would happen to me. I had never been around babies, and when my friends asked if I wanted to hold theirs I'd say, "Nope, I'm good." I thought I would nurse my infant for fifteen minutes, then hand her off to someone less newborn-averse. But no. Here I was, a self-styled badass, holder of various records for number of kills (in volleyball not the Society of Secret Assassins, but still), who strides through the world in size-twelve shoes renouncing the gooey, the squishing, the sentimental, feeling completely bonded to a tiny baby.

Even after I'd delivered her, Reece never went to the nursery. I was like, "Yo, this baby just got here, she needs to be with me." And so she was. Reece didn't sleep through the night until she was two and a half, and even though I was sleep deprived, my patience was off the charts.

This is what amazed me: I'm not nurturing in the expected way. I don't speak in a high, melodic voice to my kids; I don't honey-sweetie-baby-darling them. I don't refer to myself as "mommy." Yet here I was, nursing like some French peasant from the Middle Ages.

Before I started nursing, I planned on tapping into my inner athlete. I knew that no matter what, I had the skills to suck it up and deal with it. I wasn't expecting to be so moved by Reece's little hands opening and closing with pleasure, or her sounds of contentment. I did it for the good of the baby. I didn't expect anything in it for me. But I was surprised by the joy of it.

I'm pretty sure this is the key to contentment: lower your expectations, accept that you're going to be tethered to this little human night and day for a year and that your boobs might need a little help from the corner plastic surgeon when you're through, and prepared to be amazed.

I'm no earth mother, but I nursed in public more times than I can count. I became an expert at making a little tent with my T-shirt and shoving the kid under it. It's astounding what you become good at. Sometimes people would be talking to me for twenty minutes and they didn't even know I was nursing.

Trends in nursing change at about the same pace as hair-styles. One year everyone's flat-ironing their highlighted hair and opting for bottle-feeding, a few years later we're all wavy-haired brunettes breast-feeding until it's time to help with baby's fourth-grade science project.

But the bottom line for me was that it's good for kids, so I didn't think twice about doing it. And the shock of all shocks was I wound up loving every minute of it.

Actually, that's a lie. Not every minute. Once, when Reece was about two months old, I had a photo shoot in New York. We took the red-eye from Maui to California, where I left her with a nanny and enough bags of pumped milk to last Reece until she went to college, then grabbed a six a.m. flight and continued on to New York.

The shoot was for a fitness magazine, and there I was in some skimpy workout duds, including a sports bra. The photographer was Steven Klein, a guy I'd worked with when I was eighteen but whom I hadn't seen in a while. He hustled over and said, "Gabrielle, what is going on with your breasts!?" Somewhere between Hawaii and New York, I'd lost the handle to the breast pump, which meant I couldn't express any milk, and my breasts had become . . . overfilled. I focused on the shoot, with the goal of just getting through it. I grabbed a three o'clock flight back to California and spent half the time in the tiny airplane bathroom trying to express milk into the sink. When the plane landed the only thing I cared about was feeding Reece so I could get some relief. I cared about nothing else. I'd been awake for over twenty-four hours by now, but the only thing that mattered was getting that kid on the tit. I remember the dark, heavy sweater I wore. It was so drenched with milk the front swung around as I ran down the Jetway. When the nanny brought Reece to the gate, my breasts were so engorged, the baby couldn't even latch on.

But aside from those blooper-reel moments, breast-feeding wasn't the agony and sacrifice I thought it might be. I actually really dug it.

THE BEST ADVICE IS NO ADVICE

Mothering turned out to be easier than I'd imagined. I don't mean it was *easy*. But I think if you let go of all expectations

(I'll have my prebaby body back in three weeks; my baby will sleep through the night by six weeks and nurse until the perfect, socially acceptable moment; my two-year-old will be "terrible," but in a good way that shows he has tons of character, not in a felon-in-training sort of way; my son will love soccer, reading, and saving the planet; my daughter will love pink and ballet, or conversely black and punk rock) you'll have a better chance of landing at a place where you feel confident and good about what you're doing.

Every generation reaches middle age and starts talking about how much better it was when they were kids, and also how much worse. But one thing that everyone can pretty much agree on is that never in the history of popping out babies has there been so much crazy-making, overanalysis of the entire experience, from the instant of conception to high school graduation and beyond.

I just googled "mothering advice" and about two and a half million hits came up—that's two and a half million opinions on what you should be doing or not doing. But regardless of the advice the so-called experts proffer, all of their programs have one thing in common: they are guaranteed to make you feel as though whatever it is you're doing, you should be doing something else. This is possibly the worst place from which to parent.

Forget. All. That. Shit.

It takes a lot for me to overpunctuate like this.

Listen to your intuition. You've got it for a reason.

People who want to learn how to surf always ask Laird for

insider tips on what kind of board to get, or how to stand, or how to execute a specific maneuver. He tells them all the same thing: get comfortable in the ocean. And not just on a nice day when the waves are gentle and the sun is shining. Learn to feel at home when you've just gotten hammered by a massive wave and you're swirling around in the white water. The same is true of parenting. Everything you do stems from knowing your kids, and feeling comfortable with them, even when they're throwing tsunami-level tantrums.

The conventional wisdom is that people crave advice because they don't trust themselves, but it's really because we think that if we can find another way to do it, our days will be easier. When we stay up most of the night pacing the same five yards of living room floor, bouncing the screaming baby in our arms singing "Don't Worry, Be Happy" until we're hoarse, or spend an entire day putting a diaper back on a baby who keeps taking it off, or feed rice cereal to a kid determined to fling each and every bowl to the floor, we think: there must be an easier way—a faster and better and less tedious one.

But guess what? Being a mom can be difficult, slow, and sometimes so boring that most civilized nations would disallow it as a form of torture.

That's just the way it is.

There's a guy on Maui who's a genius at acupuncture. There are many strange and wonderful healing types who live on Maui, massage therapists and acupuncturists who seem to know much more about the inner workings of human beings than your run-of-the-mill doctor or psychiatrist. His name is

Rafael and privately we call him our wizard. Once, during a session with Rafael, I was going on in what I thought was an entertaining way about the challenges of being a mom. Rafael paused, put his hand on my arm, and said, quite seriously, "Of course, women suffer more, and because they do, they are more interesting."

THIS IS WHAT I'M FUCKING TALKING ABOUT

I hope you're not offended by my language. I have no real vices—don't do drugs, don't smoke, don't even drink. I do drop the f-bomb when I'm feeling intense about something, and everything I'm writing about here is incredibly important to me. I am committed to being a good wife, a good mother, and a good citizen of the world, which means, to me, being modern, gnarly, and straightforward. If I'm harsh and direct, it means let's get down to it.

It also means: hey, I'm a flawed human being with a limited amount of patience, doing the best I can—and so are you.

One thing that will make you feel better about whatever it is you're dealing with is to say "Are you fucking kidding me?" to yourself or your partner.

Brody seems to like nothing more than a nice bowl of sliced-up apple at three a.m. I will have finally gotten back to sleep after the two a.m. glass of water request, when there she is again, standing beside my bed in the dark, asking for the apple.

"Brody, go back to bed, you're not having an apple right now."

We tussle a little, she marches back to her room, and I say to Laird's dozing back, "Are you fucking kidding me?"

Trust me, a little bit of cussing does wonders. The later in the day it is, or the earlier in the morning, the more important this is for your sanity, and to help you feel less like an underpaid servant and more like the sassy teenager that is still lurking somewhere inside your bill-paying, car seat–purchasing, sleep-deprived self.

If you have any doubt, consider the megapopularity of *Go the Fuck to Sleep*, described as the first bedtime book for parents who live in the real world. Which, like it or not, is where we all make our homes.

NOTE TO DUDES

At the risk of contradicting myself, I do have some specific counsel for any guy dealing with a new mom. I know they probably don't want my advice, but I won't let that stop me.

The minute your chick has a baby, treat her like she's your new girlfriend.

I mean this literally. The woman has just had her whole life turned upside down, not to mention she feels like she's been turned inside out, then back again. She feels like the moment she stands up all her internal organs are going to drop straight out of her.

Don't walk in the room and treat her like the little mother, by which I mean with that deadly sense of reverence and timidity we usually reserve for people who have, against all odds, survived a tornado. Even though this is what she is.

Treat her like your chick.

Go over and stroke her hair. Give her a kiss. Ask her if you can get her something to drink. Offer to take the baby so she can shower and change into something that's not her spit-up-stained sweatshirt.

The degree to which we appreciate these gestures cannot be underestimated. It convinces us, first, that we are still the same person you at one time thought was pretty hot. Second, it reassures us that over the coming weeks and months, when we are going to be doing fucking everything (this may not be technically accurate, but every mother since Eve who was left alone to potty train Cain has hurled this accusation at one time or another), there will still be a time, perhaps after the kids are in bed, when you'll treat us like this. Nicely. Like you adore us for the women we are, and not the beast of burden we're sometimes worried we've become.

I remember being pregnant the first time and my hormones were raging in such a way that I was chasing Mr. Charming around the sofa, begging for it. The man who can stare down a skyscraper-sized wave on an average workday without blinking an eye was terrified. Who was this giant, horny pregnant woman, anyway? Three days after I had a C-section, he was sizing me up and giving me the waggly eyebrow. Having just been cut open after a day of labor (an

understatement if there ever was one) I wasn't feeling especially kittenish. Laird was polite and respectful but persistent.
The same lizard brain that had cautioned him against the
imagined danger of jostling his unborn offspring had given
him the okay to now chase me around the sofa (metaphori-
cally speaking; I could barely hobble to the bathroom).

When I went to the doctor for my one-week checkup, he
asked how I was feeling, or whether I had any questions. The
recommended waiting period for intercourse after a
C-section is four to six weeks, but my look must have said it
all. He said, "Just be sure to use a condom. Your incision
hasn't healed and your cervix is still open, so you're vulnerable to infection."

So sexy.

I was thirty-seven when I got pregnant with Brody. I was what
they call in the baby-birthing business an "older mother." I
was feeling vulnerable in a way I hadn't when I was pregnant
with Reece. There's something about having a baby on your
hip and one in your belly that makes every trip to the market
feel like a long exodus on foot to a foreign land.

The pregnancy went fine, but everything was just harder
this time around, like doing a familiar training circuit with
twenty-pound weights instead of the usual eight. Even though
Laird was onboard for another baby, I was still concerned that
another one might be one too many.

Where we lived on Maui, no hospital will do a VBAC, a

vaginal birth after Cesarean. In most big-city hospitals the procedure has become commonplace, but not here, where they're simply not equipped for such a thing. Thanksgiving is my favorite holiday, and my plan was to put on our usual big Thanksgiving spread, then fly to California and my regular doctor in Malibu, who delivered Reece and would supervise what was hopefully going to be a totally uneventful vaginal delivery.

The day before my flight to L.A. I was in our bedroom packing and from the other room I heard Laird say something loud enough to convey that it was meant for me, but not so loud that I could actually hear it.

I walked into the living room and there on the big flat-screen TV is an aerial view of our house in Malibu, encircled by flames. The flames are close enough to fry the petunias growing beside the front porch.

". . . house of surfer Laird Hamilton and his wife, Gabrielle Reece . . ." the newscaster said.

Shit is burning in the driveway, flames are singeing the side of the house.

"Are my toys burning up in there?" cried Reece.

"It's okay, Reece, we have this house. Look how lucky we are. We are here in Maui in this house, with our pictures on the walls and all of your toys. Look at everything we have."

I stroked Reece's hair while the baby was doing the backstroke in my belly, watching my house in flames. Hours later, after we'd turned off the TV, L.A. firefighters donned their superhero capes and saved our house, but at the moment it looked as if it would burn to the ground. As I searched my mind to figure out where we were going to stay when we flew back to California, it became clear that we weren't going anywhere. I would be having this baby in Hawaii. Somehow.

I was thirty-six weeks pregnant, four weeks from giving birth, give or take, and spending my days running around Maui looking for a doctor who would deliver me. It appeared that all the best OBs on the island were part of the Kaiser Permanente system, but I didn't have Kaiser. When I offered to pay in cash, they refused because I wasn't a regular patient. A friend who owns a fish market, and provides Kaiser to her employees, offered to hire me, but by then everyone knew that Gabrielle Reece was stalking the good doctors of Kaiser Permanente Maui, on the verge of completely losing her shit.

I found Dr. Christy Hume on a warm, cloudless day. She was young and unflappable and had just arrived from the mainland and was willing to take me on. I could tell by her handshake and the calm way she flipped through my chart that she was competent. Still, I grilled her about the number of babies she'd delivered. "Gabby," she said, "it's going to be okay."

Christmas came and went. Still no baby. New Year's Day morning I woke up with labor pains but I couldn't believe these were contractions; who goes into labor on New Year's Day? But we started timing them, and I called Dr. Hume and she said it sounded as if today was the day. Minutes later the phone rang again.

"Hey, Gabrielle, it's Owen Wilson, do you remember me?"

"Hey, Owen. Yeah, I remember." Owen lives on Maui when he's not on a film, and he shows up to see Laird every once in a while.

"So, where's Laird? I want to get into it."

"He's at Ho'okipa, Owen."

"And what's he doing later?"

"Well, I'm in labor right now, so I think he's probably going to be with me, having a baby."

"Right. Well, I'm trying to get ahold of him."

"You can try to track him down at Ho'okipa, if you want."

Like every woman about to have a baby, I was overwhelmed by that freakish nesting urge and decided that I needed to make some chili and corn bread for Reece and Laird, to get them through the night. Just as I pulled the corn bread out of the oven, Laird showed up, and I was beyond relieved. By then I was pretty much bent in half, and it really was time to go.

Trailing behind Laird was Owen Wilson and some friend of his—a very polite guy from Texas, who took one look at me sweating and panting and holding my belly and knew better than to say a word.

But Owen leaned against the counter and ogled the corn bread. The man had all the time in the world. "You know," he said, "that Reece, she debates me on everything. She didn't agree with one thing I had to say."

"Yeah," I said, panting, hanging on to the edge of the counter as the iron grip of another contraction seized hold of me, "that's Reece." To Laird I said, "I made some chili—"

"You know, I'm really starving," said Owen. "You don't have any sour cream to go with that chili, do ya?"

Finally Owen's polite friend from Texas convinced him it was time to go.

One of the last thoughts I had before Brody was born was that Laird and I weren't really prepared for another child. Our situation was not wholly unusual, but it was complicated. Reece was our firstborn, but Laird had another child, Bela, by his first wife, Maria Souza. I met Bela when she was four months old. Laird and Maria had joint custody, and when Bela was staying with her mom I made an effort to send Valentine's Day cards and Easter baskets, to reassure her that her dad loved her and thought of her as much as her mother did. It was hard for me. My ego was sore, all the time. I had to deal with the reality that I wasn't the first wife, and I wasn't the first one to give Laird a child. It was hard to shake that feeling of being second class.

One day when she was a toddler, Laird and Bela were in the shower, laughing and goofing off. I was in the other room, and when I heard them playing, I suddenly felt so left out. Girls so often look just like their fathers (once Reece and I ran into Laird's sixth-grade teacher on Kaua'i; she took one look at Reece and said to me, "Are you married to Laird Hamilton?"), but in one of life's little practical jokes, Bela resembles her mother.

I don't get jealous much. I'm aware how unproductive it

is, and it's usually a side effect of comparing yourself to others, which I don't do as a matter of course. But at this moment the jealousy juices were flowing. I was horrified and mortified and every other "-fied" that applies. To be jealous of this lovely little child, this innocent bystander!

I confessed this to Laird, who took it in stride. "Look, it's natural for you to have feelings around this," he said. For the Weatherman, feelings aren't that scary—they come, they go. The tide comes in, the tide goes out. I felt a little relieved: at least I could be honest.

As Bela got older, and we spent more time together, our relationship grew and genuine love developed. She's now seventeen, a thoughtful, self-possessed beauty. She gets much better grades than I ever did, but in so many ways she's temperamentally more like me than my biological daughters are. She holds her cards close to her chest like I do. She's often difficult to read. I never introduce her as my stepdaughter. Bela is my daughter.

I wasn't the cause of the breakup of her parents' marriage, but meeting me gave Laird the impetus to leave. It was a brutal time for everyone involved, and when Bela asks about it, I try to be as honest and respectful as possible. Her coming into my life was less than perfect, but the beginning doesn't matter in light of what it brought me: I'm so grateful for how it all turned out, to have Bela in my life. And I have to give her mother credit: she never tried to turn Bela against me.

Nothing teaches selflessness like being a stepmother.

Blended families are an instant grow-up pill for every adult involved.

Brody Jo Hamilton arrived on January 1, 2008.

Now we were five. Laird and Mr. Speedy, the dog, were the lone males in a house full of mermaids.

The only child in me quietly freaked out, but the volleyball player rejoiced at the prospect of living in a house with all these rabble-rousing females.

3

THE CARE AND FEEDING OF MR. CHARMING

Recently, Laird and I were invited to speak at a TED conference in Washington. TED stands for Technology, Entertainment, and Design, and is devoted to "fostering the spread of great ideas." Thousands of the world's top scientists and thinkers have given TED talks; they're completely riveting and you can check them out online. Laird and I were invited to speak at TEDMED, a spin-off of the original TED that focuses on health issues. We were going to talk about real-world solutions to healthy family living (and, yes, our kids have been known to eat chocolate for breakfast), and we were stoked.

Once our plans were firmed up, I set about doing what I always do—getting us organized for our trip. I am an organizer by nature. It makes me feel better to have things dialed in and under control, and I'd be the organizer of my household regardless of whether I lived alone or with a husband and ten children. I am the boss of the endless sometimes mind-numbing minutiae that comes with domestic life, and I wouldn't have it any other way.

The day before we flew from Kaua'i to Washington, D.C., I was upstairs packing for our trip and I heard Laird's truck in the driveway. Then I heard him bustle in, bustle out, hop back in the truck, and roar off. I was folding the shirts I know to be his favorite. The same ones I'd dragged out of the bottom of Laundry Mountain that very morning, and then washed in a separate load to make sure they were dry in plenty of time to pack in his suitcase. I was packing my beloved's shirts, with love and care and thoughtfulness, while he dashed in and dashed back out. It sounds like a little thing, and actually, it *was* a little thing, but I was tweaked nonetheless. I bust my ass at home, and I'm happy to do it, but every so often I start feeling a little too much like the house gnome. I'm fully willing to believe that I'm overreacting, but I learned years ago that it's better to risk an argument than to try to pretend something doesn't bug me.

I called Laird and asked what was going on, that I'd heard him come in. I wasn't about to pounce and blame—at least not at the moment. I'm a big believer in right time, right place. You have to do something pretty heinous to have me react in the moment.

It's something a lot of my girlfriends struggle with—feeling something deeply, but holding off on expressing it until the time is right. But seriously, if you can hang out with your feelings for an hour, or even a day, you'll have the time you need to cool down and approach the situation like a rational human being. This tends to yield better results. I'm not suggesting you repress or deny your dissatisfaction, but you don't need to react instantly.

Sometimes it's just better to hang a heavy bag in the corner of your garage and work out on that when Prince Charming is exhibiting behavior neither charming nor princely. Or call your best girlfriend and go for a long march around your neighborhood, where you can rant and rave with complete freedom.

On the phone, I could hear Laird was distracted. He was deep in one of his board designing projects, or maybe milling some wood, which is just about his favorite dry-land pastime, something he does to occupy himself until the ocean serves up some suitable swells. Really, his entire day involves keeping the ocean in his peripheral vision. He always wants to keep rolling, getting all his chores done for the day so he can get some surfing in before dark.

Several years ago Laird was a guest on *The Colbert Report*, and by way of welcoming him to the show Stephen said, "I am an admirer of what you do physically. I think it's beautiful. But I got to hammer you here a minute. You ready to ride this wave? Get a job. Time to grow up."

The audience howled and Laird threw back his head and laughed, too. It's true. People go surfing on vacation. Or surfers are teenage boys who still live at home where Mom does their laundry and their car insurance is miraculously paid for. But surfing is Laird's job. It's his career. He loves it, and it defines him, but it's also his *work*. He's spent decades practicing, perfecting, innovating.

He isn't just a surfer; he's also invented three different techniques that are so radical, they've changed the entire sport. In the 1990s, Laird and some of his friends, frustrated that they couldn't surf the huge outer-reef breaks—they couldn't get to them, and couldn't paddle fast enough to catch them—started riding out on Jet Skis and towing one another into the monster swells. Tow-in surfing was born. Now, when the ocean cooperates, he regularly surfs thirty-five-foot waves. The biggest wave he's ever snagged was seventy-five feet, then he carved across the wall of water going fifty miles an hour. Tow-in has completely revolutionized the way surfers approach the ocean.

There's a gnarly wave that breaks at Teahupo'o in Tahiti, a thick wall of water that folds itself over a sharp coral reef only twenty inches beneath the surface. Considered by the surfing world as one of the deadliest waves on earth, a wipeout means pretty much certain death. On August 17, 2000, Laird rode it, making history and the cover of *Surfer* magazine, with the caption *oh my god . . .*

But changing the course of surfing history wasn't enough for him. He went on to develop modern-day stand-up paddling, and hydrofoil boarding ("foiling"), which allows him to ride a huge swell in the middle of the ocean that doesn't even need to break.

The man is always ready. This very minute, as you're reading this, somewhere in the world, one of those heavy, world-
class swells might be brewing, and Laird has to be in peak
physical condition to ride it. In all of his appearance contracts
he has what's called a "twenty-foot clause," which excuses him
from the event if there's a wave twenty feet or taller breaking
anywhere in the world. When *Riding Giants* opened the Sun-
dance Film Festival in 2004, I flew from Maui to Utah with
three-month-old Reece, while Laird stayed behind to surf
Pe'ahi, on the north shore.

Work is work. Dentist husbands have to see X number of
patients and landscape architect husbands have to see that so
many shrubs are planted, and professor husbands have to
teach so many classes, and Laird has to put so many hours
into being a waterman. Depending on what the waves are
doing that day, he might go surfing or foiling or stand-up
paddling. He might spend all day working on a design for a
new board or tweaking an old one. The ocean is his office.

No one knows this better than I do, or understands the
kind of frustration he feels when everyday life intervenes and
threatens to keep him from doing his job. But I'm his wife,
not the hired help. And on this day, when I was rushing
around trying to get us packed for our long fight across one
ocean and one continent, his self-absorption was getting on
my nerves.

On the phone I laid it out. "Look," I said, "when have I
ever stopped you from doing what you wanted and needed to
do? I'm your biggest advocate. You know this, right? The thirty

seconds it would take for you to come upstairs and say, 'Hey babe, how's it going?' is not too much to ask."

He apologized.

Laird is one of those men who isn't afraid to say he's sorry. Which works out well for us, because I'm one of those women who, once I accept someone's apology, I'm over it.

It's not as if Laird and I knew how to make a marriage work from the stellar examples set by our parents.

Laird's birth father disappeared before he was a year old. His dad, L. G. Zerfas, and mom, Joann, met in high school, in homeroom. Her last name was Zyirek. You can imagine how it was, two attractive adolescents marooned together at the end of the alphabet. Joann was nineteen when Laird was born. There were a lot of boyfriends after that, a revolving door of guys, until Bill Hamilton came along.

Laird met his future stepdad on the north shore of Oahu. Laird was the brat on the beach, tagging along after the cool older guys. Bill, a fixture at Pupukea at the time, and also a respected designer and fabricator of high-end boards, took Laird under his wing. Bill was only maybe eighteen when Laird introduced him to his mom.

Bill married Joann, gave Laird his name, and the three of them moved from Oahu to Kaua'i. For the next ten years Laird watched Bill and his mom, whom he adored, break up and get back together. It was a tumultuous marriage, and in 1977 it ended. Joann eventually fell in love with a good man, but Laird witnessed his beloved mother endure a lot of shabby treatment for most of her life. She was a hard worker—she started the first helicopter tour business in Kaua'i—and always seemed to be involved with men who weren't. As a result, Laird is old-fashioned in his treatment of women, almost courtly.

My own parents didn't fare much better on the happily ever after front. I was born in La Jolla, California, in 1970. My father was Trinidadian, studying in California, and my mother was from Long Island and spending time there. They met at a party in Marina del Rey, stayed together for a few years after I was born, then split up. My father stayed in California, while I went with my mother. She traveled a lot for her work—training dolphins—and I spent many of my early years living with Aunt Norette and Uncle Joe, whose marriage was hiking-boot sturdy. Norette and Joe weren't really my aunt and uncle but neighbors in Amityville. Even though they weren't blood relatives, they were like family.

Norette and Joe had met when they were only fifteen. Life wasn't easy for them. They were working class, emphasis on working. I suspect I get my love of grinding from them. They arose in the dark every morning: she drove a school bus, he worked construction, and also, for a time, for the New York Department of Sanitation. They were like oxen yoked together, plowing through life like the friends that they were. Sometimes it seemed as if they were just putting up with each other, but I did witness what it looked like for a husband and wife to present an allied front.

One day when I was five I was sitting on my bed and heard the phone ring in the kitchen. Norette and Joe had a tiny house. My bedroom was next to the kitchen, and I could easily hear anyone talking on the phone. After Norette picked up the phone and said hello, I could tell something terrible had happened. My father was dead, killed in a plane crash.

I eventually moved with my mother to the Virgin Islands. She married a man named José, an attorney, with whom she shared an interest in travel, language, and food. They were passionate for each other, and for having fun. Life in St. Thomas with my mom and José was one big party; the nitty-gritty part of marriage, the day-in, day-out aspect of it eluded them.

I was thirteen when they separated. José didn't do much to create a stable environment, but he was good to me. Even after I won a full scholarship to Florida State, he sent me three hundred dollars every month. Walking around money, he called it.

By the time I was eighteen, I was on my own, and I didn't harbor a lot of high-minded hopes about ever having a working, successful marriage based on mutual love and respect.

But then there was Laird. And together—through a lot of stumbling and false starts—we've learned how to do it.

For one thing, we try to surround ourselves with people who know how to have good marriages. Not that these people don't struggle, but they're open about it. They're straight shooters.

In the same way that people who want to eat better have a better shot at succeeding when they hang out with people who eat well, spending time with couples who are making their marriages work ups the odds that you'll make yours work, too.

Laird and I are friends with a couple who disagree more than they agree. And there's none of this "agreeing to disagree" business; they go at it. We've witnessed them argue, but there's no dirty pool. There's no trying to punish the other guy for disagreeing. For us, they offer an example of how to play fair, how to stand up for yourself while also feeling you're not going to get bitch slapped for owning your feelings and opinions.

Plus, it's always good to avoid operating in a marital vacuum. How reassuring is it to know that the most happily married couples you know go through the same stuff you do? That the most squared-away, in-love husband and wife tussle over who left the last half inch of milk in the carton?

Another thing I've learned is that it's crucial to defend my marriage. Last year I was in New York and I got a call from my friend Tiffany in Kaua'i, asking if everything was okay, and if there was anything she could do. I had no idea what she was talking about. It turned out a mutual friend had gone to a class at Cross Fit in Malibu and the instructor, as part of his beginning of class chatter, mentioned that Laird and I were getting divorced.

I immediately called Cross Fit and left a message for him. I told him what I'd heard and that it was bad enough he was spreading gossip that wasn't close to being true, but that he was doing it in my neighborhood, where I did my shopping and where my children went to school. He called me back in about three minutes, and left a message, mortified. He wanted me to call him back so he could explain himself.

Yeah, right.

I'm willing to believe it may be more difficult for us because we're in the public eye, but even if we were a pair of grade-school teachers living in a cul-de-sac, and the people two doors down were talking trash about us to the neighbors, I'm pretty sure I would still march down the street, knock on the door, and have it out.

Laird and I have a solid marriage in part because we share a value system. He makes me think, makes me laugh, is an inspiration in his ability to focus on what's important to him (his family, but also being true to his own calling, and to himself), and a lot of nights we crawl into bed—such party animals are we, the lights are often out by nine-thirty—and stay up too late talking. Just talking. About what happened during our day and how that's made us aware of our good fortune, about Reece and Brody and Bela and how different they are, and how we might better parent them, about the house we're building overlooking the Hanalei River.

My life is good and I'm grateful for every minute of it and blah blah blah.

Yes, blah blah blah, because one of the truest, most mysterious things about us humans is that however much we have, however good things are, it's the little, niggling, everyday things that threaten to bring down the big, good things.

It's your sweetie's inability to keep track of the car keys, or be on time to pick up the kids from soccer practice, or failure to move the clothes from the washing machine to the dryer when he sat there and looked you in the eye and promised he would do it during halftime, that somehow winds up eclipsing his good qualities.

It really is the straw that breaks the camel's back, the snowflake that triggers the avalanche. There's a great, goofy children's book called *Who Sank the Boat?* that illustrates the dilemma perfectly. A donkey, sheep, cow, and pig all decide they want to go for a row. As each animal climbs aboard, the little boat rides lower and lower in the water. But who sinks the boat? The mouse who hops on at the last minute.

Whatever the particular issues are in our relationship, we've got to identify them and then attend to them even if they seem minor and ridiculous and petty. If something makes you clench your teeth or roll your eyes or call your girlfriends and complain like a woman unhinged, you've got to deal. You must. Otherwise, those issues will go viral and before you know it, the crumb-infested couch cushions or sopping-wet towel left on the bathroom floor has transformed into a feeling of dread in the pit of your stomach when you hear his key in the lock.

THE POWER OF THE LIST

I've found that it's essential to be clear about what you absolutely need in a partner, what would be sort of nice, and what doesn't matter at all. Doing this is easy enough. All you have to do is make a list. It's so short, you won't even need a piece of paper: name five things that you absolutely must have in a partner. If you're already married or in a relationship, list the five things you most cherish in your partner or spouse. This is really more about knowing yourself than about knowing Mr. Charming. What do *you* absolutely need?

I have one friend whose list reads like this: funny, reliable, smart enough, good in bed but not a maniac, able to appreciate art. This friend is an artist herself, so she doesn't want a partner in a creative field, but she does want someone who's interested in what she does. She's got her demands dialed in.

Me? I need my partner to be honest, possess a level of strength that's greater than my own, someone I can admire, and who's competent and confident in a specific way, someone who says, on a daily basis: Is that broken? I can fix it. Does that need to be moved? I can move it. Is that tree in your way? I can cut it down.

So, what do you need? An excellent provider? Someone who's prompt and on time even when the bridge is out or he's stuck behind a snowplow? Do you need to be the one in charge? Does your partner need to be your spiritual leader, or a great outdoorsman?

I should also say that in addition to "the five," there's a silent sixth thing that must appear on the List: physical attraction. If you don't have the urge to jump his bones, if you don't find him hot-ta-ta, you're looking at someone who can be a friend but not a partner. Don't for a minute think it doesn't matter. It's the underpinning for everything else. If it's not there, move on.

After you've got the List, tattoo it on the inside of your skull.

Then, understand that everything not on the list is open for discussion. If a guy who's up to date on world events is on your list, then that's what you have to have. If he stops reading the paper and starts logging in double-digit hours on Halo every week, you've got a problem. If, however, he lets the lawn get too long, but taking pride in the house isn't on the list, then you're obligated to find a way around it. Hire someone to do the lawn or mow it yourself or ignore it or make a deal with your husband: if he mows the lawn, you'll make those baby back ribs he goes crazy for. My point is this: everything *not* on the list is negotiable.

It's key in marriage never to feel as if you're compromising too much, because after a while you start feeling as if you're selling yourself out. If you have the List, you've got a little guide to what you'll tolerate and what you won't.

There are certain kinds of women who, you can tell by looking at them, see everything that's going on in their household and they just seem unruffled by it all. Maybe you knew one of them when you were growing up—they were the mother of a friend or a cool aunt. They were usually older, and they'd seen some things in life. This woman was tender and womanly, but also superstrong. She behaved with a kind of subtlety and grace that had nothing to do with stuffing down her feelings or denying who she was. You could watch her having a discussion with her husband, and he'd be insisting the sky was pink, and you knew she knew it was blue, but she just let it pass. I like to think that this woman was operating based on her own List, made long ago.

And by the way, it's not just us women who have to put up with less than desirable traits in our partners. It goes the other way, too.

An old friend named Robert is married to Lorrie, a woman who couldn't be on time if she was being chased by a bear. Wherever they're going, Lorrie will be late. She starts getting ready late, and then she takes too long, and then she dawdles around a bit. Instead of pacing around getting himself amped up, Robert tells Lorrie that he'll just meet her at the restaurant, or wherever it is they're headed. He goes and has a drink, or catches up on his email, or hangs with his buddies, and Lorrie shows up half an hour later and everyone is happy. She doesn't feel pressured by him and he knows the minute the date is set that she's going to be late and adjusts accordingly. Robert and Lorrie have been together for thirty-five years, and it seems to be working out just fine.

IN THE "MOOD"

The other night I was making dinner after I'd played all afternoon in a volleyball tournament. During the months we're based in Kaua'i, I spend every Saturday playing pickup games with a bunch of the local guys, but on this day we signed up for a formal tournament.

I'd had a great day and felt pumped from being in the sun and competing and just having a lot of pointless fun. I was looking forward to coming home and being with Laird and my girls. Some days I can't wait to bust out of the house and then not ten minutes down the road I start missing them.

When I got home Laird was outside on the patio, standing in front of the grill in his swim trunks and flip-flops—his normal workday ensemble—staring at the tongs and grumbling. I could tell right away that he was in one of his moods. The very same ones I used to tiptoe around.

I asked him what the matter was and he muttered that the tongs were too short or too long, too something with the length. I didn't catch it. Inside, Reece was watching TV, playing with the remote, turning the volume up louder and louder and louder. When I came in the house, Brody had been in the kitchen, asking for something to eat. I could hear the cupboard doors opening and closing, and I could tell she was warming up for one of her world-class fits. And now here was Laird, complaining about the tongs. It wasn't quite dark yet; the sky was a rosy purple. A few big Kaua'i roosters with emerald green and bronze feathers strutted over the deep green grass. I looked past the lawn to the ocean. I could just make out the white frill of breaking waves in the growing dark. Kaua'i is one of the most beautiful places on earth, and our little corner of it, on the north shore near the town of Hanalei, is one of the most beautiful spots on the island.

I felt immensely grateful. And yet . . . and yet . . .

Why was he going on about the damn tongs? This is the

dilemma and the mystery (and, okay, the opportunity) of marriage. I could hardly be luckier. I know this. I know this every day, and yet, at this very moment I could feel the pressing urge to inflict physical damage on someone. I inhaled deeply, slowly, and asked, "What's wrong with the tongs?"

"I guess I want to be as far away from the fire as possible, don't I?"

I cut him with one of my laser looks. Your run-of-the-mill stink eye has nothing on this look. I can easily cause a second-degree burn with this look.

I'm not interested in swatting the hornet's nest, but as I mentioned I made a vow to myself, back when Laird and I were on the verge of breaking up, that I would always call him on his BS. I wouldn't swallow it, wouldn't pretend whatever it was hadn't happened in order to keep the peace.

We've been together for seventeen years, and it's taken me about that long to figure out how to cope with his moods. Yup, it pretty much *is* rocket science. At any stage of the interaction something can go wrong.

If he's in a mood, I don't dance around it. I've come to learn that he resents it. So I come out pretty hard, give him one sharp poke, which is meant to say, "Hey, you can have your bad mood, and I'll even let you take it out on me a little, but there is a line."

But bad things happen fast. This is true in combat, rodeo events, and marriage. The line between a retort meant to call your guy out and a full-on scream-fest is a fine one. So I turned around and walked (I did not stomp) back into the kitchen. A few minutes later I was standing at the sink and he came up behind me and gave me a hug. That was his way of apologizing, and I let it go.

Some would argue that a hug is not technically an apology. That an apology should look something like this:

He: I'm sorry I was being a jerk just then.

She: Yes, you were.

He: I'm really sorry. It was just one of my moods.

She: That's okay. You're forgiven.

He: So, we can go have sex now?

THE SHINY EYES

Laird and I couldn't be more different, personalitywise. He's an open book, the most present person I know. If he thinks something, he says it. If he starts something, he wants to finish it, hopefully by the end of the day. I'm intense, interior. I mull things over. I ponder.

Oh, and by the way, I have my moods, too. I have half a mind to drag Laird in here right now as I'm writing this and have him sit down and tell about the time he came into the kitchen at the end of the day, put his arms around me, and said, "Hey, baby, how was your day?"

What he could not have known was that it was one of *those* days. It started bright and early with the two beloved children hair-pulling, biting, and losing important extracurricular items, and then a weird little persistent knock in the car engine and running late, always late, for everything, and several bouts of sobbing, and one of the beloved children was coming down with something, and spending hundreds of dollars at the grocery store, and then, trundling out to the car with the now alarmingly loud engine knock, and missing the curb and the cart tipping forward and the apples and oranges rolling right off the top and into oncoming traffic.

So, how was my day?

I dropped that look on him, the laser look, slightly recalibrated to say, "I blame you, even though you were out providing for us and in all ways minding your own business."

Then he jutted his chin out and gave me the look that a bull usually reserves for the cowboy he has cornered in his pen and said, "Sorry I asked."

And I, eager to tussle, said, "Where in the hell is that coming from?"

And then we were DONE. The fight was on.

But I like to think that now that I have the List, and the image of the tender, superstrong woman who knows when to let things go, I'm better about reining in my inner bitch. The reasoning is simple. I don't like it when he takes his moods out on me, so why should he be expected to suffer my wrath for things he had nothing to do with?

I've spent most of my adult life around men. All kinds of men. During my professional sports career I was a woman among men playing mixed doubles on the beach, and a woman among male basketball players, track stars, and business executives and creatives during the years I had my sponsorship deal at Nike. Now, my husband is an athlete and all his bros are athletes, too. I'm like their sister. I hang with them, work out with them, and have learned, over the years, to see their points of view. My main observation after all this exposure is that testosterone is not just real, it's *huge*.

And this realization has led to a belief that makes us chicks a little uncomfortable: men don't much like living in captivity. They allow it, they submit to it. I'm sure they don't mind having someone to scramble them up an egg and toss their laundry into the machine. But if they get to feeling too controlled, it can turn into a frog-in-boiling-water situation. And it's like, *what happened?* They ogled some cute girl at a party or tested the waters at match.com, and suddenly they're driving a minivan to a coed baby shower in the suburbs.

I'm no sociologist, but I do think that on some basic caveman level, this makes them feel rebellious. The demands of modern domesticity are not in sync with the basic hardwiring of the human male.

There they are, wearing shirts with buttons on them, getting their hair cut by an expensive stylist, and they have to be somewhere. They always have to be somewhere because their woman *told* them they have to be somewhere.

No wonder they love to go to strip clubs and throw their hard-earned money at chicks and get into general trouble. There's a lot of misogyny in the air these days. From the serious threat to women's reproductive rights, an issue most people thought had been settled decades ago, to the naming of women as a "special interest group" by certain politicians, to the somewhat silly *Newsweek* story claiming that high-powered businesswomen dig being spanked, and men love to spank them because women basically stole their jobs. Dissing women has become culturally acceptable. I wonder if part of it isn't because men are chaffing against the demands of domesticity.

The easiest way I can think of to help combat this is to remind our men that we're with them for who they are, and not because, now that they're home for the day, they can take the baby so we can finally take a shower.

To this end, I've perfected a demeanor I think of as the Shiny Eyes. When Laird wanders in at the end of the day, no matter what's going on, I put a smile on my lips and summon some shine into my eyes and say, "Hey honey." Brody and Reece might be bickering and the phone might be ringing and the toilet might be clogged, but I conjure up my Shiny Eyes. And I smile.

A lot of times, I'm *acting*.

Shocking, I know.

I don't believe in being dishonest. If you want to fight, then have at it, but if your desire is to have peace, then it doesn't hurt to let Mr. Charming know that you're actually happy to see him rather than letting loose your inner bitch-on-her-last-raw-nerve the moment he walks into the house. Switching gears from crazy mom to his chick gets me the response I want from him. When I become the girl with the Shiny Eyes, my thoughts get shinier, too, and he becomes the guy I want him to be.

BETTY DRAPER DOESN'T LIVE HERE

A friend of mine, who has seen her share of marriages that worked and those that didn't, doesn't go for the Shiny Eyes. She believes the shiny eyes routine is too close for comfort to Betty Draper, the beautiful, woman-child of *Mad Men* fame, the classic fifties housewife who was expected to pose sweetly in front of the stove, dutifully tending her spaghetti sauce in her shirtwaist with her apron on, putting on a happy face for the Mister.

My friend misses the point that I'm not doing all this because I have to, or because that's what women are supposed to do. I don't do it because it's behavior that defines femininity. I do it out of pure, modern-day, self-interest.

Laird knows that if I didn't want to be with him, I would leave. He knows I'm not against divorce—I've already filed for it once—and that if the day came when we no longer respected each other, could no longer find a way to stay connected, I'd pack my bags and go. I can easily make my own money, and since we live in two places, we wouldn't even have to divide anything up. He could stay in Kaua'i—aloha—and I could go back to California.

Every time I don the Shiny Eyes, every time I set aside the domestic lunacy that I deal with daily, it's me communicating to Laird that I'm in this. When I suppress my grumpiness, I'm saying: this is me doing my part to make this work. By choosing to behave this way, I'm choosing you, and choosing to be in this with you, and holding up my end. I'm saying, by doing my part, I hope that will encourage you to do your part.

GIVING THE PRINCE AN ASSIST

The sum total of my own List? Good, old-fashioned masculinity, which is more complex than we sometimes give it credit for. He's independent, competent, and brave, but he's also got a tender, nurturing, providing side—that's the side that brings home the mammoth.

Once, Mr. Charming was surfing the epic swells, out on his Jet Ski with one of his crew. They were run down by a hundred-foot wave, then dragged underwater for a third of a mile or more. Laird came up for air and saw that his friend had cut open his leg, a huge bloody gash. The friend would have bled out had Laird not stripped off his own wet suit and used it for a tourniquet, then swam a quarter of a mile in the rough surf to get the Jet Ski, dragged his friend aboard, got him to the beach—he's buck naked during all of this, by the way—and delivered his friend to the EMT. When Laird was done, he went back out there and caught a few more waves.

Cowboys (or their big-wave equivalents) really are my weakness.

I want to do what I can to help Laird be the kind of man I want to be with, which means creating an environment where he's free to pursue his passion and to be truly great at what he does. (Which sometimes does include being competent enough and brave enough to save someone's life.) Frankly, I don't want him to be worried about whether or not Brody's monthly fees for her gymnastics classes are paid, or whether we're out of dryer sheets. I don't want him to go to baby showers with me.

One of the weirder behaviors of women, I sometimes think, is that we fall for a guy who lives for playing his music, or mountain biking, or writing computer code, or making elaborate meals, and once we land him and settle in, what do we do? Bitch about him for playing his music too much. Or taking off on the weekends with his bros for an epic bike ride. Or staying up too late in front of the computer. Or cooking meals that take too much time or make too big of a mess. Or are fattening.

When the very thing we dug about them cramps our domestic style, we want them to spend less time and energy devoted to the very thing we loved about them in the first place, and usually the thing that makes them feel the best about who they are.

My theory, based on nothing other than my own experience, is that if we make an effort to support our partners and allow them to be themselves, to pursue the things that make them feel best about themselves, a lot of the other bullshit arguments will fall by the wayside. Yes, it may mean you need to do more laundry than you think is "fair," but wouldn't that be worth it?

Every other boyfriend I've had was less male than Laird, and also less male than I am. This probably comes as no surprise, given I'm six foot three, wear a size twelve shoe, and once upon a time could leg press 935 pounds. I'm totally capable of handling everything in my life and the life of my kids. Everything. I don't need a man in my life for that. What I do need is something different, and I get that from Laird. When I get in over my head, Laird saves the day. He always does. With him, I'm no longer the most badass in the room. I get to be the girl in the picture. That's important for me.

A funny thing happened when we moved into our house on Maui. I drew out the plans, which included where the furniture would go. We're big people, and we sleep in the biggest bed you can buy, a California King. I had to order all the furniture, including the bed, on the mainland, to be shipped to Hawaii in a container. Months later, it finally arrived, but the big wooden bed frame with upholstered headboard wouldn't fit through the bedroom door. We spent an hour turning it this way and that, angling it just so, trying to wrap it around the door frame, everything you can think of.

I'm seventy-five degrees and sunny. Nothing much rattles me. But I was about to lose it. All the money, all the time, and this gigantic bed frame was stuck in the doorway. When he told me it wouldn't fit, I just gave him a look and walked away. I wasn't even upset; it *had* to fit. There was no question.

I took a break and I went and stared at a bird flitting outside the kitchen window. And I tried to focus on its undeniable beauty and to concentrate on being grateful, rather than letting myself get bat-shit crazy over something that was not important but had nevertheless become a life-or-death issue.

When I went back, there was Laird inside the bedroom with the bed frame in place, just where I'd drawn it on the plans. He'd fetched his Skilsaw, removed the upholstery, cut the headboard in half, dragged the whole thing into the bedroom, screwed the headboard back to the frame and reaffixed the upholstery.

That's Mr. Charming for you.

THE FOUNDATION IS THE FOUNDATION

None of this—knowing the traits you require in a partner, calling him on his behavior rather than stewing or sulking, behaving like you're glad to see him, or helping him be the guy you want him to be—works if you don't have a rock-solid foundation. The degree to which marriage is a lot of work, as people like to say, depends on the strength of your foundation. If you don't share common goals, or you feel as if you're not playing on the same team, it's tough to go the extra mile. And life is full of extra miles.

So many little things can contribute to cracks and chinks in the marital foundation. Maybe you and/or your guy spend money on the sly. Or someone has a little gambling problem, or a video-game addiction. Maybe you're getting a little too cozy with your old high school boyfriend on Facebook. It's nothing huge, but just enough to make you feel frustrated, and like maybe making the kind of extra effort a successful long-term relationship often demands just isn't worth it.

Laird is a great-looking guy who pretty much lives in his bathing suit. And when he's on the beach, who is usually in his immediate field of vision? Cute girls, also in their swimsuits. I know they flirt with him, and so long as it doesn't happen right in front of me, I don't much care. I've accepted that this is part of the Being-Married-to-Laird package. I trust him. I know that if the moment ever came where he fell for some surfer chick, he'd come straight home, and we'd have it out, for the simple reason that he would despise having anything monumental like infidelity cluttering his headspace.

No, the crack in our foundation was alcohol. I don't drink, but Laird used to enjoy a bottle of pinot noir from time to time, and his drinking pounded at our foundation.

He wasn't out hitting the bars—a fifth grader stays up later than Laird Hamilton—but when he was drunk he behaved like someone I no longer recognized. Sober, he is conscientious, conservative in his risk taking, alert to danger. Drunk, he liked to haul ass around our property on Maui on his ATV, roaring over hills, catching air, bombing around like a lunatic. There were nights I was convinced he would flip over and kill himself. He went to a place inside that was wild and disengaged from the girls and me. When he drank, we were no longer a team, which is perhaps why he drank, as a way to recapture his lone-wolf days.

The problem, unfortunately, was that he was no longer a lone wolf. Setting aside myself for a moment, he was a father of three. Did he really want to do something stupid and deprive his daughters of a father?

I told him I didn't like him when he was drunk. I didn't like the part of him that revealed itself, and I didn't like dealing with him. Once I said, "Hey, maybe you can drink until the girls are teenagers, so they can see firsthand what lunacy it is and then maybe they won't do it. So at least we'll get something positive out of it."

He heard me. He knows I don't say stuff like that unless I mean it.

I would never have issued an ultimatum and told him to stop drinking, but Laird is far from stupid. He saw what it was doing to me and my willingness and ability to be one hundred percent devoted to our marriage and partnership. In 2007, he gave up his pinot noir. That helped me to feel our foundation was solid; it's what I needed to go the distance.

4

THE SECRET TO EVERYTHING

As I was putting my husband's clean underwear away, I tried to do the math. Living together for seventeen years, married for fifteen, laundry done once a week (usually more often, but we'll say weekly for ease of calculation): I've done this chore 780 times.

On occasion, I've preferred this chore to working out.

Even though I'm a fitness advocate, and even though I know that everything good in my life, and I mean everything—my attitude, moods, health, ability to be a good family member who doesn't fantasize about walking out the door and joining up with a merry band of (childless) pirates—flows from my working out and staying active, but sometimes I'd rather do anything else. Like put away Laird's tighty-whities.

People imagine that because of how I look and what I do, I bounce out of bed every morning with a twinkle in my eye and a song in my heart: woohoo, I can't wait to workout! I'd say my desire to train at any given moment is always about fifty-fifty. Yep, that means half the time I'd rather lie on the couch and eat a bowl of cereal.

I'm just like you.

Actually, probably not just like you. Probably a little more challenged in the movement department.

Fewer than one percent of American women are taller than five feet ten. I was six feet tall at age twelve, six three at fifteen. The popular wisdom is that my height must have made me some natural-born, badass athlete, but just the opposite is true. My arms and legs are so long, sometimes it feels as if I have twice as many moving parts as the average woman. Despite my level of fitness and my aptitude for volleyball, not a moment passes where I don't struggle to find and maintain my center of gravity, where I don't despair about how uncoordinated I feel in my own body. In a few minutes I'll stand up from the chair I'm sitting in as I write this, and there's no guarantee I won't trip over my feet between the desk and the door. It makes me anxious.

This isn't something new. When I played volleyball at Florida State, I worshipped our coach, Dr. Cecile Reynaud. I would do anything Cecile asked of me. I was a hard worker, tough, and serious. But during water breaks at practice she would make the team walk the length of the court on their hands, on the way to the drinking fountain. I couldn't do it.

I wouldn't do it. The thought of going up on my hands felt scarier than jumping out of an airplane. My head felt so far from the ground, and I was sure my arms would collapse and I'd crack my skull open. Cecile's solution was to stick me on the sidelines doing push-ups. It was humiliating, but I accepted it. There is no aha moment in this story. I busted out those push-ups for Cecile until I graduated.

So when I bang the drum for working out, it's not as if I've had it all dialed in from day one.

Still, regular exercise is the secret to everything. There is nothing else we do about which we can make that claim. Unless you were just rolled out of the operating room, there's hardly ever a reason not to go out for a walk. We all know that exercise is necessary for weight loss, developing muscle tone, and cardiovascular health. But the benefits just keep on coming: regular workouts prevent low back pain and varicose veins, boosts your immune system, and wards off the common cold; it gives you the glowing complexion of a chick many years younger; and gets your digestive tract on track. Exercise reduces your chance of dying young, of suffering a stroke or heart attack. It's not only a natural cure for depression, but also deals out all those great endorphins, the world's best high, natural or otherwise.

Even if you can convince yourself your abs are perfect the way they are, or you inherited your dad's naturally low blood pressure, or all the women in your family lived to be a hundred and two, there is one thing that exercise fosters that everyone can use: the feeling of being glad to be alive.

Exercise makes you happier. And even if you don't particularly want to be happier (I know a few people who groan and complain as if it's a sport), it will make you more even-tempered, and thus make everyone around you happier, which will make everything else in life *easier*.

In a perfect world we'd be able to connect to all these reasons for making exercise a priority, but in the end, whether we're aware of all the benefits or not is irrelevant. I once wrote a magazine article in which I tried to lay out all the good reasons, the smart scientific reasons, for working out and I wound up just saying, "Screw it! You need to work out because it makes you look hot."

And still, how many of us say, I want to look hot, I'm dying to look hot . . . after I eat this cupcake.

And I'm no exception.

One morning I was minding my own business, answering my emails, and one of them said, "Sorry about the magazine." *Magazine? What magazine?* This couldn't be good. I emailed my friend back and learned that some checkout counter tabloid had done a story on the cellulite to be found in certain celebrity booties, and there was mine.(You would think that knowing strangers were out there evaluating my ass would be enough to up my desire to train to at least, say, seventy-thirty, but no.)

The worst thing was that someone had Photoshopped my backside to look fatter than it actually is. To retaliate, I took a picture of myself in my underwear, posted it on my website, and blogged about it, saying here's the unvarnished truth. At least let's be honest.

I've tried to train myself not to let this type of thing get to me, and mostly I do a pretty good job. People are going to say what they're going to say, and now that we have the Internet, they can say it at any hour of the day or night, and if you're really in a self-sabotaging mood, you can check it out for yourself.

I ignore it all, for the most part, but for some reason this time it really got to me. I locked myself in the bathroom. Took the longest shower in human history. Why was this getting to me? I took a little inventory. I noticed that because I was extra busy I wasn't getting the time I needed to work out. I had been on the road and was out of my routine. Had I been exercising, I wouldn't have been so upset. So once again I was schooled: exercise is the secret to everything.

THE SECRET TO THE SECRET

There is, however, a secret to the secret: figuring out your strengths and weaknesses and arranging your life to support the strengths and make it inconvenient for the weaknesses to prevail. The gold standard of examples: if you keep Pringles in the house you'll inhale them, if you don't, they're out of sight out of mind.

The only thing that separates me from you is that I'm well

acquainted with my weaknesses, and rather than eradicate them, I simply try to deprive them of oxygen. I know what to do in order *not* to support them.

In 2003, after I had Reece, I immediately saw that I wouldn't be able to hit the gym any old time I pleased. It was one of the first reality checks of motherhood. Suddenly, I was beholden to this tiny, helpless creature, and her needs didn't adhere to a convenient workout schedule.

What to do? I knew my weakness—if left to my own devices I'd slack off and get my workouts in only half the time. But I also know I'm someone who, under the right circumstances, can kick her own ass harder than anyone else.

So, I created a home gym in Maui, where we were living at the time. It wasn't fancy—I bought some weights, kettle bells, a physio ball, and a yoga mat—but creating that space was my commitment to myself. It meant that even if I had my kid sitting there in her baby seat, or even lying on the floor next me, cooing and amusing herself by waving her arms and legs in the air, I was going to be able to exercise. After the gym was equipped, I invited some people to come work out with me. At first, maybe three people showed up.

In April of that year, when we moved back to California, I was able to borrow the home gym of a friend. To make it even more fun to work out, and more likely that I wouldn't skip a session, I put out the word that I was going to be doing some serious training on such and such a day, and about ten people showed up.

After a few months we were fifteen, and I had to start getting organized. Every morning before meeting up with my workout buddies, I sat down and wrote out a circuit, a dozen or so moves that gave us a full-body workout.

October came, and we moved back to Hawaii, this time to Kaua'i. We rented a house in Princeville, on the north shore, not far from the St. Regis hotel. The guy who ran the gym there invited me to use their facility, but since none of my workout friends would be able to join me, I said thanks but no thanks, and found I could rent out a small room at the local community center. My friends would join me, but my class would also be open to the public. Word got out, as it tends to do on the sparsely populated north shore of Kaua'i. The class was free, but there was a prerequisite: you had to commit to working hard. The class grew; on some days there were about fifty people, almost always all women, with the occasional fearless guy who would show up to check it out.

Here's the routine: Fifteen minutes before class I load up the bed of my pickup with all of my free weights, kettle bells, Versa bands, and sound system and drive the short distance to the community center where my women stand waiting to unload the equipment. Then we press ourselves into the small room, I demonstrate the moves du jour, separate my women into smaller training groups of three, crank up the music, and start working, hard. My circuit isn't difficult, but it *is* demanding.

Some of my women show up three days a week, week in, week out. Sometimes someone comes up to me after class and wants to pay me, or otherwise do something lavish to show her gratitude. I tell her, she's already doing it, by inspiring me with her commitment. There's nothing that I need that I don't already have, except people to inspire me. When my women show up day in, day out, with their great attitudes and great energy, they don't realize that that's their gift to me.

Showing up three times a week, being committed, is the most I can do for them, and I'm lucky to have the opportunity to do it. In a superficial way, I'm not getting anything in return. I'm not getting paid, nor am I getting PR.

What I *am* getting is a chance to practice the Code of Laird. In Malibu, during the summer, his off-season, Laird devotes a lot of time to his workout group, which consists of ten dudes who train six days a week; three days a week they circuit train, and three days they work out in the pool. Laird is the leader, the innovator, the instigator.

In October, when we decamp for Kaua'i, he leaves those guys behind and rejoins the Hawaii crew. Not an hour after our plane has landed and we've dropped our suitcases in the house, he's found Terry Chung, Kaua'i's stand-up board manufacturing guru, and off they go, surfing and foiling and redesigning boards along with the rest of his surfing crew, and here, too, he's the leader, the innovator, and the instigator.

His greatest gift is the ability to be present. When he's in front of you, he's in front of you. It's ten-thirty on a Tuesday morning and you're hanging out down at the barn with Laird and you express an interest in going down a waterfall: let's go. Want to go over to Na'Pali? Want to go stand-up paddle? He's there, he's your man. The flip side of that is when he's gone, he's gone. He's not going to call to check in with you, but he doesn't love you any less. You just have to wait for him to come back. And he will.

I try to live by the same code. When I'm training my women I'm there, one hundred percent. Even though five minutes after we're done I have to race to take Brody here, or Reece there, or do a Skype meeting, I'm not there. I'm here.

One time I wasn't feeling well and was thinking about calling off the training session and Laird laughed and said, "Oh no, the Rock's going to cancel? The Rock always shows up." The other day I had a volleyball game on the same day we were scheduled to train. I wound up arranging for the game to be played later. The Rock never cancels.

And there's one other thing. One of the moves I've incorporated into my workout sessions? Handstands! You couldn't pay me to do them back at Florida State, but at age thirty-seven I swallowed my fear and did one with my heels against the wall; now I do them every time I train. Well, most of the time. Say fifty-fifty.

NOW IS THE TIME

Working out and getting and staying fit doesn't have to be beastly or daunting. When I was a kid growing up in St. Thomas, people got exercise by swimming and walking and riding around on their bikes. Most people could probably have been more fit, but I'm sure their general level of fitness overall was much higher than that of many contemporary folks who vow to themselves that tomorrow they're going to start working out two hours a day while, at the same time, nourishing themselves with water and lettuce leaves, until they have quads of steel and glutes like Mario Lopez.

Of course, tomorrow never comes.

If you haven't worked out for a while, it's as easy as this: start walking. Can you walk at a good pace for twenty minutes? Add ten more. Maybe you work out two days a week for thirty minutes. Could you add a day? Could you go for forty minutes? The point is to do more, and to continue doing more, but not in a way that intimidates you.

The key is finding a way to introduce these new habits into your life with a sense of reality. It can't be torture. It can't be something that makes you utterly miserable. You can't feel deprived and pissed off because of it. You can't feel like "Oh my god, this is *one more thing*." Aim for mild, aim for gradual. Aim for an activity that you might come close to enjoying.

It doesn't matter if you're doing eight reps with two-pound weights or if you danced around your living room while your kid is in the bouncy chair. All that matters is that you had a great time and challenged yourself a little.

THE EVERYDAY 100 PERCENT

Exercise physiologists have recently discovered that the person who exercises for thirty minutes with intent and focus gains more from her session than the one who dials it in while texting or reading a magazine, or simply not paying attention.

When you work out, whether it's two or three or four times a week, for fifteen minutes or for an hour, do it with purpose. Be there, just for that time, one hundred percent. I've probably spent years, all told, in the gym, and I see it all the time: people show up with their trainer and they're jibber-jabbering, catching up on gossip and just not paying attention to what they're doing. You can't multitask when you're training. You can't be somewhere else in your head while your body is here working.

It was bad enough when gyms stuck TVs on the ceiling in front of the treadmills (a lot of gyms now have Cardio Cinemas, basically movie theaters where the seats have been replaced by Stairmasters and other machines) and made sure there was a fat collection of recent magazines by the ellipticals. Now we've got our phones, which can and do provide an endless opportunity for distraction.

They've not only become our electronic security blankets, they also allow our bodies to be in one place, while our heads are somewhere else. I'm here with you, but I'm also texting. We tend to work less hard when we're watching a movie; we also tend to be less aware of our posture and body alignment, which can lead to injury.

Oh, I know. Some days it's murder to get yourself to exercise, and if you didn't have the promise of a movie or a mystery to occupy yourself while on the treadmill, you'd skip it altogether. And pretty much all trainers agree that anything that will get you to commit to a regular exercise program is better than nothing.

They're one hundred percent correct.

Whatever gets you through your workout is all right.

But I'm an optimist. I believe that if you pay attention to your body during exercise, you'll wind up enjoying yourself. When you exercise, for that relatively short amount of time, put the phone in your gym bag. Unless you're expecting a significant communication regarding a loved one or a big work-related thing, you don't need it. And never hire a trainer who allows you to keep your phone nearby or to chitchat.

When I work out, I work hard, and I work the people I'm training hard. I consider this to be part of my work life, even though I'm not getting paid for it. I show up and I'm on time and I do my job. I'm a little tough on them. I yell at them for talking. We're not here to gossip. We're here to work, and maybe to have a laugh or two. We do intense intervals of squats with weights in each hand, stationary lunges, jumping jacks, push-ups. But we also take breaks. Twenty seconds of brute hard work, five seconds of uninterrupted rest. Anyone can commit one hundred percent to an exercise for twenty seconds, knowing that the rest break is coming, literally, in a matter of seconds.

Bottom line: your workout regime shouldn't be overwhelming, but you must also accept the fact that it's not like getting a massage. It is a form of work. When you go to the DMV you don't think "this is going to be awesome!" But you go because the outcome—tooling around in your car (legally)—is important, and even necessary.

TO COMMIT, CONNECT

Let's consider, for a moment, a hamburger. In order to be hot and in shape and all of that, you don't have to give up the things you love. But if you're having a burger for lunch, can you eat half and wrap up the rest to take home?

Here's a trick: once you've ordered it, ask the server to take the other half away and put it in a to-go bag. (Seriously. Get rid of the half you're saving immediately. Don't let the mofo sit there tormenting you.) Savor what you're eating for lunch. Take a bite and actually taste it. Eat it slowly and eat it without a smidge of guilt.

And when you go for your walk, feel your feet, your legs, and hips. Feel your butt. I don't care if you're a hundred pounds overweight. Start getting connected to your body. Fitness isn't about being in perfect shape and a size six.

When I train, it's not with the goal of showing the world I have killer abs after having had two babies, or to look good in some dress I'm going to have to wear to the next social event. I train to feel connected to my body, to feel my muscles work, my joints move in their sockets, my breath travel through my lungs.

At least once a week after a training session a woman will come up to me and tell me that after the workout she feels more stable, more balanced, and more confident. This is why exercise is the secret to everything; it's the secret to making you feel connected to the way your body moves in space throughout the day.

One fortyish woman I work out with is in good shape and comes to class regularly. Still she's beginning to develop that curvature of the upper spine you see in older women—dowager's hump, as it's charmingly called. One day after class I pulled her aside and told her that her exercise routine was all well and good, but her homework every day was be aware of her body outside of class. That she needs to consciously remember to use the muscles in her upper back to pull her shoulders back, and to make sure her head was balanced over her neck, and not jutting forward. I could see that she felt a little frustrated by my suggestion. I told her about my lousy knees and how pretty much every day I'm managing knee pain. As we get older, we've all got our crosses to bear. My goal is not to be a muscle meathead, but to experience vitality, enjoyment, and longevity.

I've been holding my classes now for several years, and every last one of my workout buddies has gotten stronger and gained stamina. But our bodies are smart. They adapt. Once the work starts to feel easy, you're not going to get the same results. Only minutes into the circuit I can tell when my women are complacent.

My solution: step it up. Rather than doing each move for twenty seconds, I increase it to a minute. I up their weights. I add another round to the circuit; instead of doing two sets, we do three. This way, we also get psychologically stronger. At the end of one minute of push-ups you think, halfway done! I'm only going to see those fuckers one more time. But to know they're coming around twice more, and each time you'll be a little more fatigued, that's tough.

But my gang knows enough not to complain. They know my philosophy by now, that it's good to feel a bit uncomfortable. As the saying goes, life is lived just outside our comfort zone. In my own training, I like having to come face-to-face with my own character. When I play volleyball, even though it's just on the weekends with a bunch of the local boys, I enjoy the pressure. These are the moments when we get acquainted with ourselves.

HURRAY FOR THE GOOD OL' GIRLS CLUB

One Wednesday, at the end of the group workout, one of my women approached me with a bag full of avocados. If you haven't had Hawaiian avocados, you're missing out. They're big and buttery and can be chopped up and tossed into salads and smoothies. I'd run into her once at the market and we'd chatted briefly about how the Reece-Hamiltons love their avocados, and clearly she'd remembered. I was touched.

And I realized then that my circuit group was about more than just working out, that it was also about providing an environment where women were able to connect, that our commitment to come and sweat in unison was a kind of relationship, even though none of us were friends (either in the real world or the Facebook sense). But we're all working together, we're working hard, and we're helping each other. What could be better?

When I meet women who don't like other women, I can

sense it right away. The stereotype of mean girls is rooted in a sad reality, and women need to be conscientious about supporting one another. But part of supportiveness is being straight. Say I have a friend who's having trouble with her partner. It might seem like the friend thing to do is to jump with her on the he's-such-an-asshole bandwagon, to agree in all ways that he Done Her Wrong, but really, my job, as her friend, would be to help her see what's going on with him. Real women will love you enough to tell you straight.

We're more likely to develop that side of our personalities if we do something constructive together. Sure, hitting a shoe sale can be fun, but taking a walk is better. It's good to have a collective goal, which is why sports for girls is so crucial. Men gather around a task, women just gather.

Then, after we become mothers, the first thing to fall by the wayside, besides caring whether we have spit-up stains on the shoulders of our T-shirts, is our friendships. If we do have time to hang out with other women, they are usually moms who have kids the same age as our own. And what do we do with these new friends? Bitch and moan, usually. Trade war stories about ear infections, sleepless nights, our husbands. The same old, same old, and nothing that's very uplifting.

But start training with a group of women, and suddenly you find yourself with a dozen or more new pals. Maybe you're not "friends," strictly speaking, but most likely you don't have time to devote to real friendships anyway. And better yet, the contact you have with your training posse is all positive, all the time.

The community on the north shore is small, and I'm always running into my ladies at the market or the beach, and we have nothing but fond feelings for one another. We have a quick chat, promise we'll see each other at the next session, and the good feeling of having interacted with another chick in a positive way lasts the rest of the day. We don't have to spend hours small-talking or gossiping. It's completely sufficient for me to ask, "How's it going?" I've genuinely contributed to her health and well-being, and she's inspired me by her willingness and energy. I don't have to strive to find a different way to connect, nor do I have to fake a connection that isn't there.

It sounds corny, but playing volleyball all those years really did teach me a few nonsport-related life lessons. Among them: a female is actually capable of having another female's back, even during times of strife. I had conflicts with my teammates all the time, but during a match we were still able to put our differences away and support one another. Women don't have a reputation for being able to do this. It's all personal, all the time with us. Our emotions run the show and dictate how we act with one another. But once you play on a team for any length of time you learn to put aside the disagreements when it matters, and one girl's success becomes another's.

Likewise, I learned early on never to measure myself against another teammate. There were always going to be girls who were bigger, stronger, and faster than I was, and girls whom I was bigger, stronger, and faster than. I realized I had to just do my thing, and work hard at what I knew I was good at. When I saw a chick that was a badass, my goal was to acknowledge it without being threatened by her talent or her power.

One year I played on Team Nike with Natalie Williams, an NCAA player of the year who went to UCLA and lettered in both volleyball *and* basketball, and went on to play in the WNBA. She was six one, one ninety, and biomechanically perfect. We would close the block and she'd bump me with her massive shoulders and *boom*, I'd be on the ground. Once, I played volleyball with a girl from the Virgin Islands who had a thirty-two-inch vertical leap. It goes on and on.

I think it's important for women to get that attitude going, where we can celebrate one another for what we excel in, without comparing or competing. It's ugly when we pull one another down, and it does nothing to improve the quality of our lives. And in the same way it's self-sabotage to envy people; you should strive not to feel smug when you're obviously better than the person next to you—that's poisonous in its own way.

I always remember the old saying, "comparison is the death of happiness."

Over time, my circuit-training group has learned to root one another on. On any given day we all know the ladies who are enjoying a good patch. Their training is going well, they're full of energy, they're smiling, and they look great. Their success is contagious and for those of us who are dragging our sorry asses around and trying not to clock watch (just because I write the circuit doesn't mean I'm immune to sucking at it from time to time), they are a joy. This kind of interaction is part of my personal code. I always want the group to be about the greater good.

I train women from seventeen to seventy. I give them all the same circuit, with a few suggestions on how they can modify. I want the seventeen-year-olds to grab a bigger weight, and the seventy-year-olds to be mindful of their backs. I want one of the fifty-eight-year-olds, who is more ripped than I am, to keep pushing, and keep enjoying herself, for years to come.

It's important for me to train people of all different ages. I'm not suggesting that an exercise group can take the place of your family, but it's rare to see three generations under the same roof these days, and as a result we have a low tolerance for anyone who's not exactly our age, who doesn't have a child the exact same age (preferably in the same grade), and who doesn't like the same clothes, food, bands, and home décor.

Training together gives younger chicks the chance to work alongside older women who are serious about their fitness and see that life (and lifting) doesn't end at age thirty-five. The rest of us thrive in the presence of the young ones, especially when they're confident and working hard. It's a reciprocal relationship that creates respect.

Of course, you shouldn't exercise at the expense of spending time with loved ones; however, if you're taking care of your physical needs, the quality of that time will improve. And in the end, isn't it about the quality of our relationships and experiences, and not making sure all our emails are answered and the laundry is perfectly folded?

My friend Katie Hester, a onetime federal judge with a southern drawl, is always full of wise, down-home advice, and she says, "Don't invest in 'things,' but rather in relationships and experiences."

My experience has always been that if you invest in your own physical health, your relationships and experiences become even more healthy, happy, and sweet.

5

THE KEY TO LIFE IN THE KINGDOM OF FOOD

My standing weight is between 170 and 172. In college I weighed between 140 and 150. When I competed professionally I weighed 163. When I was pregnant with my daughters, I weighed, yes, 200.

My point? Like every other person living in the first world, I'm aware of my weight. I also love food.

I have asked my friends who have become vegans, "Don't you miss meat?" They say, "Nope, tofu is so much better." I have asked my friends who have sworn off sugar, "Don't you miss chocolate?" "Nope," they say. "Never even think about it, and I feel so much better!"

That's not me. Even though I live in Malibu, I'm not one

of those people for whom kale chips are a genuine substitute for barbecue potato chips. I love red meat and chocolate bars and ice cream and French fries. I love the Sweet Factory. All those bins of sour green apple belts and gummy worms that give you contact diabetes just being in the store? I love all that shit.

Still, I like feeling better in my body more. We all have self-sabotaging mechanisms, but my desire to survive and excel is greater than my desire to shoot myself in the foot.

This has lead me to employ (most of the time) a set of attitudes that allow me to eat well without feeling like I'm depriving myself, while still maintaining a healthy weight. And, by the way, it's not all blueberries and smoothies around the Reece-Hamilton house. Not five minutes ago I came home from working out and ate a handful of chocolate almonds.

Still, I feel I have the true key to eating well.

I'm going to tell you now, in case the mere mention of food and nutrition is so stressful it sends you mad-dashing to the nearest Dairy Queen and you think it would be better for all concerned if you just skipped ahead to the next chapter.

Not that I would blame you. Alcoholics can give up whiskey and tweakers can swear off meth, but we've all got to eat. Food—especially bad food—is a drug like no other: it's cheap, legal, and everywhere.

So we're up against a lot. Added to which, women, especially wives and mothers, have been trained to put everything and everyone else first. Which means we're at risk for eating whatever's handy (hello, Pringles!).

Anyway, the key is this:

When you put something in your mouth, always know why you're doing it.

Are you genuinely hungry? Do you just need to feel something crunchy and salty in your mouth? Have you found yourself at the best Italian fine-dining restaurant in New York craving the risotto? Is it one day before your period and you cannot possibly shove enough snack-sized Snickers into your mouth? Are you eating that maple bar because your children are driving you bat-shit crazy and you need to pacify yourself, right this very minute?

Eating this way prevents mindless food shoveling, which accounts for the accumulation of thousands of calories you don't even taste. It also allows for the possibility that you might find the food rich enough or filling enough, or even disgusting enough that you're good after a few bites.

So, if you're going to eat that triple fudge salty caramel brownie, really eat it. Stop texting, give it your full attention, lick your fingers, sigh, and moan. Enjoy the hell out of it.

ON DIETING

Don't do it.

I don't care if you're eighty-seven pounds overweight.

The problem with other people's diets (South Beach Diet, Atkins Diet, Zone Diet) is that it's another person's diet. Sure, these diet plans work for some people, there are a lot of people in this world. But these diets don't and won't work for everyone, and in any case, not for long. All the science points to the fact that more than eighty percent of people who lose weight regain it—and yet, we keep thinking that the answer to our nutrition issues are out there, instead of inside our own bodies.

YOUR OPTIMAL DIET IS SPECIFIC TO YOU

There are a few basics of good nutrition. The best diet is rich in fruits, vegetables, whole grains, healthy fats, and lean protein. But the exact combination of foods that help your brain and body thrive will be unique to you. What makes some people feel energized makes others feel lethargic. What hits the spot for some people is a huge miss for others.

No one knows your body better than you. Not your doctor, not your mother, and not the author of whatever diet book is currently atop the bestseller list. You're the commander in chief of your body. How do you feel after you eat a plate of spaghetti? Does the phrase "food baby" come to mind, or do you feel pleasantly nourished?

Experiment with your diet. What protein, carbohydrates, and clean fats taste good and make you feel good? Are you sleepy after a meal or do you feel energetic? Does a bowl of oatmeal for breakfast keep you feeling full until midmorning, or are you hungry again in an hour? Is a container of Greek yogurt a nice snack or does just the mention of the word "yogurt" make you want to hurl? Notice the quality of your sleep, notice how easy it is to fall asleep at night, and how easily you wake up in the morning. (Surely I'm not the only person on earth who's experienced the Ben & Jerry's Chubby Hubby hangover.)

Right eating is based on what tastes good, what satisfies, but also is influenced by genetic makeup, your height, weight, health, activity level, and age. You should experiment with your protein, carbohydrate, and fat intake.

Yes, fat. We need fat in our diets, and we need it every day.

But not any old fat. Clean fats are the healthy fats that give us improved brain power, regulate hormones, help us thrive in stressful situations, and give us pretty hair. Clarified butter, coconut oil, avocado oil, and nut oils are all sources of clean fat, and if you don't consume enough of them you will be perpetually hungry and never feel satisfied. Consuming too little of the good fats can actually contribute to overeating.

COMFORT FOOD IS NOT A DIRTY WORD

Food should taste good and make us feel good. It's part of why humans were designed this way. Sex feels good so that we'll keep the human race going, and food that's good for us tastes good, so that our bodies will be well nourished and continue to serve us during our (hopefully) long and healthy lives.

If you were raised eating fantastic-tasting pasta everyday of your life, and you associate heaping plates of lasagna with love, family, friends, and warmth, is a low-carbohydrate diet like Atkins *ever* going to be right for you?

Nope, nyet, never. Because to cut pasta out of your life is to sever you from your happy memories and your feeling of what it is to live a good life.

CHANGE ONE THING

Eating well is not complicated. A common fallacy about living healthy is that developing proper eating and exercise habits is complex and difficult and we shouldn't expect to see results right away.

While it's true that there's a period of operating in good faith, just as there is when you begin an exercise program, the day you begin to eat better food is the day you start feeling better. That night you'll probably be able to sleep better. The next day you'll have more energy. Over all, you'll feel better.

You also don't need to initiate some convoluted eating regimen. Just a few small positive changes in your eating habits, combined with a moderate level of routine physical activity, can lead to immediate measurable improvements.

Look at it this way: there are approximately 540 calories in a Big Mac, 450 calories in a medium order of fries, and 310 calories in a large Coke. People routinely order this for lunch and you can wolf it down in a few minutes. That's 1,300 calories.

Instead of a burger and fries for lunch, try making yourself a healthy meal replacement shake made with banana, yogurt, maple syrup, almond milk, and protein powder. A maple banana smoothie is just 284 calories and it tastes like dessert. It costs less than an average fast-food lunch, is more convenient, and, of course, much better for you. (Sound like too much work? Even a turkey sandwich is a better choice.)

This one change, giving up the daily ritual of a fast-food lunch, can reduce your caloric intake by over 1,000 calories a day. Since there are 3,500 calories in a pound, just replacing one fast-food meal a day with a healthy protein shake would have you on the road to losing two pounds per week. And that's if you change nothing else about the way you eat.

And once you start eating better and feeling better your palate changes. The Big Mac that once had you salivating starts to taste like what it is: a highly processed, high-fat, high-sodium, low-grade consumable specifically created to produce what the food designers call "mouth satisfaction," and nothing more.

FEEDING THE MACHINE

Maybe you don't need to lose weight, or maybe you've reached your healthy weight. Or maybe your basic diet of chocolate muffins, Hot Pockets, and cheese pizza has left you feeling icky and irritable from one day to the next.

If your weight is not at issue, your focus is feeding the machine.

The human body thrives when, in combination with daily exercise, it's fueled with exactly the right number of calories in the proper balance of protein, carbohydrates, and clean good fat, combined with the correct amount of vitamins and minerals.

If you eat at least two servings a day of fruits and vegetables, combined with a lean protein and a moderate amount of fat, on a regular basis throughout the day, your metabolism will adjust to this predictable high-nutrient diet, and you will become a calorie-burning machine.

Pay attention to the eating behaviors of the fittest people you know, they feed themselves all the time (men and woman alike), because their bodies burn the calories, and they need extra nutrition to perform at their best.

Do they eat junk food? Of course they do, but in small doses.

The basic approach is to eat healthily throughout the day, and only when you're hungry. Lots of fruits, vegetables, and lean protein, and don't keep eating once you are full. Use basic common sense. Everyone knows eating fast food every day is simply just a bad idea. Most fast-food restaurants are not far from a grocery store; it's just as easy to run into the market for a turkey sandwich and a banana as it is to grab a Whopper.

GET IN TOUCH WITH WHAT WORKS FOR YOU

When it comes to eating healthy, there is no such thing as a perfect person. We all have cravings for foods that are not so good for us. We all have at least one thing we love to eat that we would be better off without. But life is for living, and eating our favorite food is part of it.

There's no reason to banish the foods you love. In fact, you should make a point of eating the foods you love. You should worship the foods you love! Just enjoy them in moderation. If you adore French food, make a ritual of making it once every other Sunday. Make sure your *gateau de crepes* is served with a vegetable and salad and you're good to go. Giving up the food you love doesn't work, so don't even go there.

And while we're on the subject of French food, why *don't* French people get fat? Spend a single day in France and the reason will become immediately clear: they take time to enjoy what they eat. They love their cuisine, and they savor it. They take time to shop for it, to prepare it, and to eat it. They eat smaller portions, and don't snack. Although McDonald's has invaded France, and the French do love "McDo," as they call it, for the most part, you won't find them inhaling the 1,300-calorie Big Mac meal, or anything resembling it, on a regular basis.

Bottom line, your diet is *your* diet, and the foods you love are the foods you love. Just learn to control the quantity, in combination with regular exercise, and include a supplement program if you don't have the discipline to eat the right amount of protein, vitamins, minerals, and nutrients your body needs to thrive.

80/20 RULE

Around our house we have an unwritten rule: if you eat healthfully eighty percent of the time, you can go crazy the other twenty percent of the time. The concept came from Paul Chek, an exercise kinesiologist friend, who specializes in high-performance training.

A regular day at Reece-Hamilton World Headquarters looks something like this: we are a smoothie-for-breakfast family. We make 'em all different ways, but the most basic involves frozen berries, a banana, ice, maca (a root plant that helps the immune system), bee pollen, and whey protein. These smoothies are robust, about five hundred calories apiece, and get me through the morning. Lunch might be a stir-fry or a slice of cheese on sunflower bread. Dinner is some kind of animal protein, a green vegetable and/or salad (a recent favorite includes heirloom tomatoes, steamed green beans, and hard-boiled eggs), and maybe some quinoa or sweet potatoes. Generally, bread and fried stuff isn't part of the routine, but if I go to some great Italian place you can bet that I'm going to enjoy it.

Full transparency: we do have a sweets drawer filled with tubs of dark chocolate–covered almonds, caramels, and toffee. I don't indulge very often, but my girls are allowed to choose something from the drawer on a daily basis. I believe in moderation, and am not about to turn candy into a forbidden fruit by getting hysterical about it.

Living healthy requires some consistent level of self-control. You need to embrace healthy behaviors at least eighty percent of the time and reduce potentially destructive eating habits to just periodic indulgences or celebrations. It's easier than you might think. Try to use your favorite treats (those on the unhealthy side of the spectrum) as rewards for positive behaviors. If you like a big, thick cheeseburger with fries, establish this high-fat fix as your reward for not missing a single workout in a full week.

Think about it: you eat twenty-one meals a week, or close to it (not counting snacks), you can easily afford to splurge on a cheeseburger and fries, especially if you have exercised at least an hour a day all week.

Similarly, tell yourself, if I eat ideally for the next three days, the following day I'll treat myself to my favorite lunch or dinner with a friend. That's nine good meals to one not so good. This reward system is highly effective and helps keep the more negative elements of your diet under control. And it's not punishing.

A friend of mine loves cupcakes, cookies, and pies. She could easily organize a religion around lemon poppy seed Bundt cake. Passing up the Snicker display at the checkout counter is easy; she has a much harder time saying no to the chocolate chip on offer at Starbucks. So she's made a new policy for herself: she can have cookies any time she wants. She just has to make them herself. Since she doesn't normally keep chocolate chips or pounds of butter in the house, this means she has to make a special trip to the store.

Most of the time going to the store and making the cookies and cleaning up the kitchen doesn't seem worth the effort. So she passes. This keeps her from lunging for the cookies when she's bored or tired or hungry for something else. But for her, knowing that she can have those cookies any time is a comfort. Also, without any heroic self-control (which only works for a while), she's put the kibosh on one of her old habits: buying a pack of chocolate-covered graham crackers and wolfing them down while watching a *House* marathon.

ELIMINATE WHAT'S WORST

Last year a study was conducted at the New Balance Obesity Prevention Center at Boston Children's Hospital to find out which diets worked best and why. One of the discoveries of the experiment was that regardless what diet you follow — traditional low calorie, Atkins style, or low glycemic — hyper-processed carbohydrates make you fat and contribute to disease. One of the studies author's, David Ludwig, said, "If you take three servings of refined carbohydrates and substitute one of fruit, one of beans, and one of nuts, you could eliminate 50 percent of diet-related disease in the United States."

That statistic is mind-boggling. Especially when you consider that, in the great scheme of things, it's pretty easy to dump the chips for a handful of raw almonds or pistachios, trade out that scone for a banana with peanut butter, or substitute black beans for fries. Health and longevity, here you come.

The reality is that a lot of us simply don't want to change our bad habits. And why should we? It feels good to be rebellious, to thumb our noses at all this healthy eating bullshit. And we *should* indulge from time to time. Life is for living, and part of living is saying, on occasion, to hell with it.

Here's me: I will never give up chocolate. Ever. And I'm not talking about the seventy percent cocoa, one hundred percent organic, fair trade, free range, pure and holy antioxidant rich dark chocolate that's actually good for you. I'm talking Snickers. I have no other vices (unless you count dropping the occasional f-bomb) and I won't apologize for my chocolate.

But we all can change one or two things about ourselves. Take a moment for a reality check, look at the way you live your life, and honestly consider what is the one thing you do that is most contrary to a healthier you, and eliminate it.

For most of us, just changing our worst behavior will be life transforming. Are you an extreme coffee drinker? While there may be some genuine health benefits associated with drinking coffee in moderation (reduce depression, lower blood pressure in some people), if you start your day with three or four cups at home, then fire up the coffeemaker the moment you arrive at the office in the morning, then again after you've returned from your lunch break, you're not doing yourself any good.

The result of extreme coffee drinking is fatigue, lack of endurance, loss of muscle tissue, and, over time, more serious health issues (think about what this does to your stomach lining, for starters).

Cut back your coffee to two cups and your life will be transformed. If you're able to make those two cups in the morning you'll even have a shot at getting a good night's sleep.

Late-night snacking is another thing that gets a lot of people into trouble. Popping a few caramels at ten p.m. is an excellent, guaranteed way to pack on the pounds. In fact, I have friend with one of those fast metabolisms who was losing weight during pregnancy. The simple prescription from her doctor? A milkshake at midnight. Sure enough, my friend began drinking a chocolate shake before bedtime and the pounds couldn't pile on fast enough.

By taking in all those extra calories, every night, night after night, you're training your body to store fat. You don't give your body the time it needs to do all of the repairing and restoring it wants to do at night because it's dealing with calories it doesn't need. You wake up feeling groggy and unrested, and in the long run, you wake up feeling . . . fat. So just close the kitchen after dinner. Wipe down the counters, turn off the lights, and leave.

(PORTION) SIZE MATTERS

The simplest, most effective, single tactic to avoid overeating is to put only the proper quantity of food you need to eat on your plate. If you have cooked more than you need at that moment, before you eat, put the rest in the fridge or freezer for another day. Once the extra portions are stored away, it's a lot less tempting, plus more work, to get that extra serving. This is particularly important if you are a good cook, or if you have one in your family. If it tastes great, you are going to want more. That's just natural human behavior.

Many restaurants build their reputations on offering great value, which generally means you get large portions for a low price. Given that monster portions aren't going away any time soon, it's good to get into the habit of sharing with a friend. Or as we discussed with the example of the hamburger, ask your server to put half of the food in a to-go container prior to bringing your food to the table. This behavior of saving half of your meal for another time eliminates temptation, reduces your food cost, increases convenience, and, most important, helps control calories while still allowing you to eat what you enjoy.

TIMING COUNTS

While losing weight is mostly a matter of calories in versus calories out, when you eat is still important. Basically you want to try to give your body the right fuel when it needs it. You don't need a huge high-calorie dinner right before you spend eight hours snoozing.

Around here we say "eat early and often." Start your day with a good breakfast every morning, and then refuel throughout the day. It doesn't have to be fancy. A banana and a swipe

GABRIELLE REECE

of peanut or almond butter on a piece of multigrain toast is good enough. And there are plenty of nutrient-rich, high-protein, low-fat smoothies and shakes you can keep in the fridge and grab on your way out the door.

BE YOUR BEST ADVOCATE

I was about to write "Don't Be Your Own Worst Enemy," but part of the reason why so many of us have issues about food and weight is because we've endured a lifetime of don'ts. I could list some of them, but I want to get away from that negative old song.

Think of the care with which you feed other people. Doesn't your own body deserve that same respect and affection?

Show yourself some mercy.

Defend your right to take care of yourself, to carve out time, every day, to eat consciously and get some movement in. If one of my kids had a fever, of course I'd forgo a workout or grab some take-out instead of cooking, but everything and everyone else can take a number and get in line.

Forgive yourself for your imperfections. Or celebrate them—they're part of what make you *you*! The road to better health is not going to be a straight one. There may be times when your healthy eating habits go belly-up (and you notice your own belly is starting to go, er, out), you start skipping your workouts, and return to your old extreme coffee drinking, late-night snacking, chocolate-covered graham cracker

94

inhaling ways. It happens to most everyone, so never feel guilt. Even professional athletes will have weeks, even months, where they just let things go. Believe me, I'm no stranger to a plate of fries.

But it's okay, we all need a break sometimes from being disciplined. It's hard to maintain healthy eating habits year-round, especially given the demands of work, travel, special events, holidays, even your own fluctuations in mood. So expect a few setbacks, accept them, and move on.

The real problem is not reverting to old behaviors for a week or two, getting so depressed or mad at yourself that you abandon your good habits. You decide, in effect, to just give up. Or you actively punish yourself for failing to be perfect.

It doesn't matter how many times you fall off the wagon or for how long, as long as you return to your healthy habits. In the end, it's about the long haul.

ENJOY YOURSELF AND RELAX

Food is a critical part of making a house a home, and it's how most families connect. Shared meals are a chance to relax and enjoy the company of those you love. So don't let your concerns about losing weight or getting proper nutrition detract from those important, wonderful moments.

When children are part of the equation, it's especially important not to make food a divisive issue. Instead, make healthy eating a way of life for the entire family. If you demonstrate healthy eating behaviors, your kids will follow. If you have an apple at four o'clock, they'll see that as a normal snack and want one, too.

So if a morning shake becomes your routine, let your kids have some; they are bound to get more nutrition from a shake than from a processed cereal. Kids need a healthy meal to start the day, so make proper nutrition in the morning a routine behavior for the entire family.

KEEP IT SIMPLE

There is no better time to make a few positive changes in your daily routine than right now. You will get no benefit from waiting. That doesn't mean you have to go on an all Grape-Nuts diet and start training for a marathon. For many people, it's as simple as cutting back on hyper-processed food and getting into the habit of exercising a little each day.

I know a woman nearing seventy who's vibrant, smart, and still rockin' the skinny jeans. She's an avid movie buff and takes a major trip abroad every year. Her blood pressure is low, as is her cholesterol. Her big secret? Avoiding fried food and taking her Daily Twenty, as she calls it. Yup, that's all. She keeps her tennis shoes by the front door, and rain or shine, she takes a twenty-minute walk around the neighborhood every day.

That's how simple all of this can be. You don't have to let

food and exercise make you crazy. As long as you know the basics, and develop good habits, a healthy lifestyle will simply become part of who you are.

Think of food as the fuel that determines how that precious body of yours thrives and give it the quality it deserves.

6

LOSE THE PEA

Just the other day I saw a boy on a scooter making his way down the street with his mom running alongside as if she was a secret service agent attending the presidential motorcade. The boy was wearing a helmet, knee pads, and elbow pads. He was rolling along at a snail's pace. The street was flat and empty. Would it have been a huge calamity if the boy fell off his scooter? Probably not, but this mother was acting as if she was afraid for his life.

I'm all for safety, but I'm also for teaching my kids to take intelligent risks.

How could I not be, given who their father is?

Laird is the original Take-Your-Daughter-to-Work guy. It

can be a little hair-raising. One of his favorite things to do is to take the girls with him when he goes surfing. He drives his duck boat out, drops anchor, and they sit in the boat with their life jackets and juice boxes and Mr. Speedy and they watch him catch wave after wave after wave. They always love to go, and after ten minutes they're always bored. Laird paddles up and they say "Come on, Dad! We wanna go!" And they go back and forth a little and they "let" him have one more ride. Then he rides another one and he paddles up and says, "That wasn't a very good one, I need another one." And they say, "Nooooo!" And they go back and forth a little, and again, the girls let him have one more. This can go on for hours, with them sitting in the little dinghy, rising and falling in the swells.

One day Laird was down at the surf barn doing what he does down there, designing new contraptions, hacking down trees, shooting the breeze with his crew, and just being Laird. That day, he was watching Reece and her pal James. He wasn't hovering—thank God—as they ran around and got muddy and tried to climb the banana and avocado trees. The barn sits on the banks of the Hanalei River, and Laird's main focus, in that there was one, was keeping the kids out of the water.

On the other side of the barn is a steep hill newly cleared of jungle. It's slick and muddy and dotted with jagged rocks and the huge splintered roots of banyan and kapok trees. Laird was standing by the barn, at the bottom of the hill, chatting with a neighbor. Suddenly, some bit of movement caught his eye and he looked up at the top of the hill—which is maybe three hundred feet high, with a forty-five-degree incline — and there was Reece standing on a big, corrugated metal shingle, speeding down the hill. James, her friend, was sitting behind her, and they're both screaming with delight. "Gabrielle, when I say Reece was hauling ass, I mean *she was hauling ass*," Laird told me later.

"How did she get the shingle?" I asked. I was in the kitchen wiping down the counters, doing everything I could not to spin around and get all up in my husband's grill.

"I don't know, she got it on her own," he said. "I've got a pile of it by the side of the barn."

"How did she get it to the top of the hill?"

"She walked it up there herself."

I suppose I gave him one of my death stares, or maybe I just kept pretending to wipe down the counter. I've completely repressed the memory, because the next thing he said was, "I looked up and thought, Oh my god! They're gonna get impaled on those roots."

"You could have kept that to yourself," I said.

Even so, I want this sort of thing to happen. It must. How else do children learn? How do they learn not to be complete idiots, to take this risk and not that one? How do they learn how much getting hurt, well, *hurts*?

In general, dads are the best at teaching kids intelligent risks. Because moms are always like, "Oh, be careful. Do you have your mittens? Are you warm? Is your coat on?" And dads are like, "Sure, go for it. But don't come crying to me if you get hurt."

After Reece and James got to the bottom of the hill, they wanted to go again. And Laird allowed it. Only this time, he insisted they take a shorter, flatter, less rock- and root-strewn route, where he could easily get to them should something happen. But nothing did. Other than that our girl and her friend had a blast, and gained a little bit more confidence about how to be in the world.

My girls couldn't be more different. Once, at a friend's pool, Reece, then seven, spent the entire afternoon jumping off a fifteen-foot ledge into the water below, then scrambling back up and jumping again. Brody was interested, but she wasn't ready to commit. She climbed to the top of the ledge, then back down, eased herself into the pool and swam over to the spot where Reece landed. After three and a half hours, as we're packing up our towels and sunscreen and saying our good-byes, Brody decided she was ready to jump. She was only four, and part of this was her urge to keep up with her sister and the older kids, but at bottom she's also simply a deeper thinker. She needs to stand back and look around and take some time to draw conclusions about the safest place from which to jump.

I loved watching them at the pool that day, loved watching how they worked it out for themselves. Sometimes I had to close my eyes when they jumped, but I would never deprive them of the opportunity to do this scary kid stuff, ever.

Their dad is an expert at creating that place where they

can take chances and flirt with a trip to the emergency room. He provides the training wheels for a little danger, allowing them to see what it's like to live through something exhilarating and scary, and in some cases having made good choices that build confidence.

Modern moms are known for being able to do pretty much everything. We can help with math and throw the baseball back and forth in the street and shoot hoops in the driveway. We can change the oil in the car and comparison shop for health insurance and get the water heater replaced. All this we can do. But some things only dads can do. And we can't, and shouldn't even try, to barge in on whatever that special thing is their dad has to offer them.

Sometimes Laird takes the girls and their friends out on the Hanalei, and tows them around in our kayak. The kids go crazy, laughing and shrieking and exploding off the back and into the water. Yes, they wear life preservers, and yes, it's done in a controlled fashion, with Laird doing a lot of mugging and pretending he's zipping down the river like a maniac. If there is one thing Laird is not, it's foolhardy. He knows exactly what he's doing.

Both Reece and Brody are well aware of who their dad is, and what he does for a living, and he would never say to them, "You can't be part of the wild world because you're a girl, or because you're just a kid."

Laird and I want our girls to be a little tough.

We have no interest in raising princesses who can't sleep because there's a pea beneath the mattress.

*   *   *

Our children are their own people. This was true from the moment they were born, but it doesn't really sink in until they're walking and talking and refusing to wear the purple T-shirt and knocking their bowl of perfectly baked sweet potato onto the floor.

We all understand this, that our children are not possessions, but we are also quick to pigeonhole them, to claim to know who they are before they've had a chance to show us.

You see it all the time. A mom notices that her son likes to stack blocks, and forty-eight hours later he's enrolled in some pre-pre-preschool mommy-and-me architect-in-training program.

A daughter likes to sing to herself in her crib. Her parents see this as evidence of profound musical gifts. Look out Juilliard!

Perhaps all this lunacy comes from the fact that having a child is a mind fuck on such a basic level—here's me, here's you, we have sex for seven minutes resulting in an entire me-you human—that we need to figure out who and what they are as soon as possible to calm our existential selves.

But parenting our kids means getting accustomed to this dynamic where they're always unfolding. Not just growing up and into who we presume them to be, but *becoming*, morphing not once, but again and again, all through the years.

Reece spent her entire infancy sobbing. I don't think I'm exaggerating. Every time she woke up during the night, or in the morning, or even after a nap, she was crying. When she was walking, and old enough to get herself up from her nap, she'd stand at the top of the stairs and wail. I'd be on my way up to get her saying, "Reece, I'm right here. I'm *here*," but it didn't matter. A friend once said that every time her baby daughter yawned, just when her mouth was open the widest, she got this perplexed expression on her face like, "Hm, why is my mouth wide open? It must be time to scream." With Reece, I think the tears started to flow in her sleep, and that woke her up.

This went on until she was three years old. I remember thinking, how is this crybaby my child? But I didn't try to fix anything. I just let time pass and took care of her, and she grew into a girl who's up for any adventure with little concern for her personal comfort. As long as there's the chance of some fun, she'll sleep on the floor and in the morning brush her teeth with her finger. Where did that sobbing little baby go?

SIMPLIFY, FAMILY EDITION

Simplify is the concept de jour when it comes to adult lives; why don't we apply that thinking to the lives of our children? For starters, kids need to go out and play . . . for hours on end . . . every single day.

Every study you care to name says the same thing: sitting in front of a screen for too long makes kids cranky and fat. Hell, it makes *me* cranky and fat. Reece and Brody get only an hour of electronics a day. Electronics is defined as anything with a screen: watching TV, playing games on the computer or on my iPhone. If it was up to Laird, all of it would be thrown out the window. Of course, he leaves in the morning; he isn't the one who has to tell them "no" every fifteen minutes.

We adults check our phones after a meeting and before we get in the car, after we get out of the car and head into the house, after we stir the pasta but before we chop the onions, after we get up in the morning and before we hop in the shower. All these little moments, these little gaps between one activity and another, when you might otherwise enjoy a little daydream or think about a new recipe you want to try or have a thought about a book you've read or just look forward to the weekend when you're going to go snowboarding or hang with a friend, all those moments have been gobbled up by our compulsion to check our devices.

It messes with your head, and I don't want it for my kids.

So I say no. A lot. And tell me I don't feel like a shit mom when little Brody, who's been cooperative all day, has a meltdown in the afternoon and sobs miserably, "I. Just. Want. My. Electronics."

I often think my real lifestyle role model is Norman Rockwell. Throw on some jean shorts, play in a tree, throw a rock.

Is there anything more beautiful than that?

Why, yes, there is: a children's birthday party that could never be mistaken for the Queen's Diamond Jubilee. One of the things I love about living in our little town in Kaua'i is that the basic requirements for a kid's birthday party are: kids, cake and ice cream, and presents. It's a different world in

Malibu. When I take my kid to those parties with the different activity stations, and the clown and the face painters, I can't help but think, *are you fucking kidding me?*

For Reece's last three birthdays we took her and some pals go-karting. We found a great little place where the maximum speed on the cars can be adjusted down for the kids and up for the parents, so everyone has a blast. All these little kids roaring around the track. Some food, some drinks, and some cake — simple, but still with the sense of an occasion.

Halfway through the last party one of the kids turned in his kart and came over to me; he told me he had to leave early and I thought he'd come to say thanks for the nice time. Instead he said, "So, if you have any gift bags, I'll take one."

Seriously? This boy had just spent two hours in a go-kart.

"Listen, you're seven years old. Your gift bag was getting to drive a car," I said. "Now get out of here."

I'm sure his mother is still telling the women at her craft parties what a bitch I am.

A lot of us have confused good parenting with overparenting. We think if we're in our kid's faces and business twenty-four/seven, that we're doing a better job than the moms of yore who told their children they'd better go find something to do or else they'd find them something. (Every person I know over forty has the same story: one day I sighed that I was bored and in the blink of an eye I was pulling weeds or sweeping the floor.)

But even as toddlers and preschoolers, children need to feel as if they own their experiences. They need to be let out in the yard to discover worms and flowers, to pick up a snail, and, yes, to eat dirt. When they're older, they need to be free to ride their bikes and explore in the neighborhood. They need to be free to make their own discoveries. And by the way, it doesn't count as a genuine discovery if you stick a caterpillar beneath their noses. Interesting, maybe, but engineered by you, the parent.

We have to be there for our kids. At the same time, we have to get the hell out of the way.

Reece once complained to Laird that he never came to her riding lessons, her ballet or gymnastic classes.

He said, "Do it awhile, then I'll come."

He's not particularly interested in watching her learn how to point her toe. These activities are for her, to try some things out and learn what she likes and what she doesn't like, to figure out what she excels at, to get to know herself.

Do I expect her to become a prima ballerina or ride a Kentucky Derby winner? Of course not. I'm all for cheering her on, for telling her she can do anything she chooses. But there's determination and optimism, and then there's reality. I joke with Reese, "You can do everything, but I can promise you that you'll never be a professional gymnast, or a professional jockey. You can still ride horses and do gymnastics, but there's no arguing with physics." And we laugh about it. She's the daughter of a six-foot-three father and a six-foot-three mother. She's only eight and she already weighs ninety pounds.

Reece's activities are obviously quote unquote enriching, and no doubt kids learn lessons from things they take up in grade school and then lose interest in about the same time they pass their driving tests. But how about activities that are a little stickier when it comes to parental hopes and dreams? How about if you were a tennis player and back in some unlit tennis court of your mind you have a fleeting image of you sitting courtside at some big match (okay, Wimbledon), and your kid is playing in center court, and . . .

I know. We all try not to live vicariously through our children. Still, it's a tough one, realizing deep in your heart that what your child does is for her, not for you.

Not long ago Reece got the jujitsu bug. She begged me to take lessons. If Reece were a river she'd be one that flows year-round, century in, century out, eventually creating a grand canyon. She does not let up. Just one lesson? Please? Just to see? Pretty please? Just one, on the easiest day it is for you to take me? Preeeeeeeeety pleeeeeease?

The girl wore me down. I told Reece I would buy her two months' worth of classes, but once she started she would need to go until the class was over. Her brief fling with jujitsu is a chance for me to school her about keeping her promises and honoring her commitments. To my mind, that's my parental duty. I'm a lot less interested in her becoming the world jujitsu champion. Which isn't to say that it wouldn't be nice for her to have a black belt tucked into her tool kit.

Learning about dedication and commitment are the main benefits of participating in any kind of sport. I've done many talks at middle schools, high schools, and sports camps and I always say, "Listen, if none of you play in college, it doesn't matter. You are doing something valuable for yourself right now. The point of doing it is discipline, self-esteem, working with others, and working toward a common goal. All of these things will enhance you."

Being an athlete also allows a kid the opportunity to gain self-knowledge.

Who am I? What do I need? What makes me happy? I ask myself those questions, and I want to raise children who ask them, too. To be able to answer those questions is to know what is worthy of your time and sweat.

If there's one thing you can count on, it's that life rewards those who work their asses off. Think about the successful people you know. Did they all put in late hours and weekends and eat/sleep/dream whatever it was they were chasing? Even Mozart, a genius and a child prodigy, practiced like a mad fool.

Hard work is humbling. It forces you up against your limitations every time. It keeps you honest. It keeps you human.

My kids are little, so I don't know for sure, but I don't think my world would be rocked if one of them announced she decided to go to law school. It wouldn't raise my opinion of her. I wouldn't think any more of her than if she said she was going to be a muralist, or a human resources person at one of those corporations where it's hard to understand just exactly what it is they do.

Throughout my career I've done some TV hosting and color commentating. I was good enough that it was suggested I try my hand at sports announcing. But a great announcer is a critic. You have to look at an athlete's performance and take it apart. If someone hasn't brought their best game, you have to call him or her on it, and explain how they're sucking, and why.

I just don't have that in me. I appreciate people for just being out there doing it. Even if they are stinking up the court, I am happy they are there. We just put emphasis on the winner, but it's as important, if not more so, just to go for it.

I feel the same way about the things my children do. I will judge them—and yes, we judge our kids, just like we do everything and everyone else—by how hard they work to attain their goals, and by what kind of people they are. Do they have friends? Do they have manners, which is a form of expressing empathy and gratitude?

When Reece invites her friends over to our house, I'd say one in three says "thank you" and brings her plate to the sink after we eat. And I say to Reece, "Who do you think is going to be invited back here? Who do you think I'm going to cook for again?" Of course Reece knows the answer. I tell her that I want her to be that kind of person: the polite one who gets asked back.

There's a beach volleyball player named Kerri Walsh who's one of the best players in the game. In 2004 she and her partner Misty May-Treanor won the gold in Athens, followed it up with fifty consecutive match wins, then returned to Beijing in 2008 to take home the gold again and then in 2012, they did it yet again in London. Between 2005 and 2007 she held the AVP records in both hitting and blocking, and in 2007 was named the FIVB's Best Offensive and Most Outstanding Player. Her rap sheet goes on and on.

Once, during a big tournament, about fifty players were sitting around in the player's tent and there was a big metal garbage can in the center that had fallen over. No one did anything about it, thinking, I suppose, that someone working the tournament would happen past and pick it up.

Then Kerri strode in, fresh from a match. Spying the garbage can, she picked it up and started refilling it with all the trash that had spilled, the empty cups and food wrappers. The guy who told me this story reported that they were all instantly humbled and embarrassed. Here was one of the best players in history, and is she "Yo, assholes! Look at me, Ms. Three-Time Gold Medalist!"? Nope. She sees what needs to be done and she does it.

Kerri lives not by the code of fame or wealth or even hard-won achievement, but by her own code. If my daughters grew up to be like that, I'd consider myself a success.

THIS IS NOT THE UNITED NATIONS

I believe in power-parenting. I'm the parent, and I've got the power. This is similar to the Golden Rule. I've got the gold, so I make the rules.

I'm only half kidding.

I feel as if sometimes we need to say to our children, "Look,

I am in charge. I am the parent. And with that comes huge benefits for you. I am not asking you to be my friend and give me advice. I am not asking you to solve my problems, or clean up after me, or pay my bills, or take me to the doctor. I, on the other hand, am here to I create as much freedom and fun for you as I can, to give you a childhood without worry. But that is not a childhood without duties or responsibilities."

I am tough and very direct with my children. When I see nonsense, I don't launch into a big goopy speech about how I understand why they feel the way they must feel, and why they're doing what they're doing, and how their father and I don't believe in whatever it is they've just done, but we appreciate why they did it and blah blah blah. Not long ago I was standing outside the market and saw one little girl refuse to share her cherries with her sister. The mother started in with, "I imagine that when I tell your father about this he'll be disappointed in your decision to make the choice to refuse to share." Her daughter looked up at her like, "What in the hell are you talking about?"

I just say, "Cut out the nonsense."

Kids know what you're talking about.

Part of my attitude reflects my parenting credo, but part of that is just who I am. In all the hubbub surrounding being a parent, we can lose sight of the fact that we're still exactly who we were before we brought kids into the world.

I'm not a big overexplainer or coaxer or let's-hug-it-out kind of person. I don't have that light, effervescent spirit that a lot of mothers have (and which, frankly, I envy). Why would I be someone else with my kids? Why would I want to model for them the importance of being someone else, fabricated from tips gleaned on the Internet?

Brody, age four, could give a seminar on talking back. Not long ago I let Reece borrow a pair of my stud earrings. She went into the bathroom to use the mirror to put them on and dropped one down the drain. Laird was due home soon, and I thought I'd let him do the honors. Reece, dutifully, got out her markers and construction paper and made several very sternly worded signs warning that no one should enter the bathroom or use the sink.

A few minutes later Laird came home and I told him about the earring and as he opened the bathroom door Brody scurried over and threw her body in front of him. "If you go in there I'm going to smack you in the balls."

Another mom might have pulled her daughter over and sat her down and said, "Sweetie, let's talk about why you're talking like this." And they would go on to have a conversation about what happened. But that's another kind of mom. I told Brody to knock it off, that talking to her dad—or anyone—that way was disrespectful.

Of course, I thought it was funny as shit.

When Laird and I had girls, we thought, "Aw! Little girls! We'll have to protect them." But by the time both of them were four we thought, good luck world.

I suspect it's easier for the mothers of easy children to justify the adult, conversational approach to discipline. Maybe if my girls were less like their father and me, I'd try this tactic, too. Just sit them down for a nice, cozy girlfriend chat about why they shouldn't pitch fits, pinch and slug each other, break stuff, tell their little girl whoppers, tattle on each other, and all the other stuff kids just naturally do.

Laird wrote a book called *Force of Nature* and that pretty much sums up the character of Brody, also known as the Most Strong-Willed Child God Ever Put Breath In.

Brody is a fighter. She loves a good tussle. She's a complicated little being. We call her the Cat of the House. If you approach her for a kiss, she won't have anything to do with you; if you're busy doing something else, that's when she'll want to snuggle on your lap.

Once, she bit Reece *and hung on*, like some little pit bull. Even though she's the older sister, and twice the size of Brody, Reece is a lover not a fighter. She won't defend herself. I pulled Brody off her sister, spanked her, and sent her to her room. Then marched outside, where I stood by the side of the house and wept. What kind of monster was I? At that moment Laird drove up in his truck. He hurried over. What was up with me sobbing by the garbage cans? I told him what happened and he was nonplussed. I was comforted by his lack of alarm. He rubbed my back and said, "Haven't you ever seen mother lions cuff their cubs?"

I am aware of how little say I have with Brody. Her fierceness surprises even me. In order to get her biting under control, we made a contract with her; when she misbehaves, she can choose either a spanking or a time-out for her punishment. She stood there in her little shorts and bare feet and bright yellow banshee hair and considered this. She's not one to simply react.

"How hard will you spank me?" she asked.

She wanted me to give her a sample of what she was in for. Because she'd much rather have the spanking than the time-out, because a spanking is over and done with, and then she can go about her business. A time-out doesn't hurt, but it's drudgery, and that's the last thing she wants.

Only a few hours before writing this I pulled Brody aside and said, "Listen, you've been a bit rude lately, and you are not listening at all. Also, you need to stop fighting with everyone about everything. I want you to know that I'm going to start pulling on your ear a little."

Another child might have been instantly afraid or alarmed by this, but Brody was intrigued. "What do you mean?"

"When you bite people, or are very rude, I'm going to give your ear a little yank. And I'm also going to give Katie permission to do it, too." Katie is our babysitter.

"Really?" said Brody.

"Here, I'll show you." I gave her ear a tug.

"Owww," she said. She rubbed her ear, but she was completely calm. She was still more intrigued by this new development in our interactions.

"Only it will be harder. And I want you to think about this before you bite someone, or pick a fight, or are rude to us."

"And Katie gets permission, too?" she said.

This is what I deal with.

A WORD ABOUT COLLEGE

Part of being a good parent in these modern times is creating a childhood that positions our children to get into a top college.

Not.

Or at least not around here.

I want our kids to be kids as long as possible. My friend tells her college-age daughter to venture out and have fun and explore and experiment. Make some mistakes, and go down this path, no this one, no this one, wait! Go ahead and take a year off to live in Peru. Because, as my friend says, in this life we're old for a really long time.

Take my four-year-old to be interviewed for a prep-school-track kindergarten?

Kill me now.

College is terrific, don't get me wrong. My college experience was invaluable. I wouldn't have had my volleyball career without it. But part of our job as parents is to raise contributing members of society. This isn't the same as driving your offspring through four years of college, as if they're cows on the range.

The truth is: college is awesome for some people but not for others. If it's not for you, it's lunacy to rack up six figures in debt trying to stuff your square-peg self into the round hole of higher education. And just cruising through four years of course work and partying to earn a business degree doesn't float the boat anymore, if it ever did.

A better education is one that teaches kids to look for opportunities, to scan the world and find a space that only they can fill. Neither Laird nor I come from money or privilege. Everything we've achieved has been through hard work, persistence, and, yes, a lot of luck. Being able to recognize an opportunity and seize it is a key skill; we want to teach our girls that skill, and also the value of hard work. If they leave our house knowing their strengths and weaknesses, their genuine interests, and how to work hard, we have faith that they'll succeed.

PARENTING IS FOR ADULTS

Our kids are going to grow up no matter how we parent them. Also, they're pretty resilient. The planet wouldn't be groaning with so many humans if we weren't.

I try to parent my children in a way that's in sync with my personality. When we don't trust our instincts, when we act in a way we think we're "supposed" to, when we start thinking that someone else has a better idea about how to be a parent to our children than we do, we do nothing but add to the crazy stress of family living.

As someone said to me just the other day, "Stop 'shoulding' on yourself."

Laird has an interesting perspective on the whole thing: our kids are going to get older and taller and turn eighteen no matter what we do. For him, the parenting journey is for the parents. How do you function on no sleep? How do you function when a little baby is screaming her head off for weeks on end? How do you function when you must put your child's needs, always, endlessly, before your own?

Parenting teaches us all, finally, to grow the hell up.

7

BEAUTY AND OUR INNER BEAST

Not long ago I showed up for a magazine shoot and the photographer, upon seeing me, stopped in his tracks, widened his eyes, threw open his arms, and exclaimed, "Gabrielle, I am amazed at how good you still look." He's a genuinely nice person in a field filled with sometimes not-so-nice people, and it's possible he regretted that tiny word "still" the second it tumbled out of his mouth, but he went on to overcompensate, praising the state of my skin, "even though you've spent so much time in the sun," and my figure, "even though you've had two kids."

He meant well, and yet every sentence he uttered dead-ended in the same place: even though I can still rock a magazine spread with the help of Photoshop, I am not the hot-ta-ta boffo babe I once was.(Please hear the sarcasm, dear reader.) I am, like everyone else in the world, getting older.

I'm forty-two as I write this; by the time it's published, I will be forty-three, closer to forty-five than I am to forty. Some days I catch a glimpse of myself in the rearview mirror of my truck, without my sunglasses, and I'm shocked. The Hawaiian midday sun is like HDTV. I notice a new line beneath my eyes. Or I twist my forearm a certain way and see that the elasticity of my skin has decreased.

And you know what my next thought is going to be, but, sister, I'm not going there. I am not going to think it. It's counterproductive, it doesn't serve me, and it doesn't make me feel good. In this regard I follow the teachings of Meryl Streep who said, "Put blinders on those things that conspire to hold you back, especially the ones in your own head." I don't need to say anything to myself, ever, that involves the phrase "old bag."

Even the way my clothes fit is beginning to change. People think that because I can walk around in my running tights, and maybe take my shirt off and there's my sports bra or tank top, that somehow I've managed to cheat the determined demon known as aging, but I haven't. My body is changing, just like everyone else's.

GET REAL

Age is coming for us all. And the question is, do you want to take it on the chin and be grateful for your health and vitality, for the ability to move your body and partake of life, or do you want to be bitter and self-conscious and spend your time, energy, and money worshipping at the altar of plastic surgery? This isn't to say there aren't procedures out there that can make you look better, fresher, and, yes, younger—for a while. Then, you start looking like a woman I see at my local market in Malibu from time to time, who looks not young and vital, but like a sad, panic-stricken not-young woman who has had so much work done, all she is managing to convey to the world is her fear and insecurity.

Everyone turns fifty. (I should say, if you're lucky you turn fifty, because I have some friends who died in their forties.) The stark fact is that you can spend all your time, energy, and money having fat removed from this place and injected into that place, having different pieces of skin tucked and sand-blasted smooth, and other parts puffed up and light-ened. Mind you, I'm not for a minute saying you shouldn't do this. I'm not whatever the plastic surgery version of a Luddite is. The day may come when I spring for an eye tuck. Still, it's good to be sane about it, to pitch your tent in the camp of aging gracefully, and to realize that however much you have done, there will come a day when you're going to look like a really rested forty-year-old who has had work done, but you're never going to look twenty-two. That ship has sailed.

Perhaps you're reading this and thinking, "Oh, it's easy for her to say. She's six three" (not always a stupendous and ob-vious advantage; try being a five-foot-tall seven-year-old) "and has worked as a model." You're right, but perhaps not for the reason you might think.

Being in the business of being recognized for your looks teaches one great lesson: this is not something you've worked to create; it's an accident of birth. I was always more interested in the parts of my life over which I had control, and being tall and photogenic was not one of them. When I had people ogling me, I thought, "This has nothing to do with me, which means I have no use for it."

Discovering volleyball in eleventh grade gave me a sense of purpose. It was something I could do, and do well. And after getting my ass handed to me on the court a few times, I learned that you may be sixteen and rocking that pair of shorts, but if you're playing badly and you keep missing the ball, you basically suck. The shorts, and how you look in them, don't matter. The reality check is immediate and brutal.

Once, when I was still playing volleyball at Florida State, I turned down a lucrative, weekend modeling job in New York because it conflicted with a match. How I performed in my sport was important to me, whereas having my picture taken simply didn't. It never seemed like a real job to me. Of course I pursued opportunities I felt were worthwhile, but through it all, I always remembered that my core value wasn't based on how I looked.

Over the years this attitude has allowed me to keep my head on straight when, for example, people start asking whatever happened to Gabrielle Reece? Whatever happened to the once Top Most Beautiful Hot Woman in the Known Universe by a Glossy Magazine with a Huge Circulation, only not to be named, or mentioned, ever again? The subtext of these "whatever happened to" questions is abundantly clear, to you, to your friends and family, and to the world: once young and gorgeous; now, not so much. There's no room for the luxury of self-delusion.

Youth is a currency. Beauty is a currency. But let me tell you, it's a currency with a limit. And if you can't figure out a way to transcend that, it's a slow, miserable death.

Sure, there is a certain amount of mileage you can get out of being pissed off. But it won't carry you that far. And it won't make you happy.

After my circuit training class on Wednesday there's a no-sweat class. (This is Kaua'i; people live most of their lives here beneath a dewy sheen of perspiration, so I assume this means a gentle yoga class.) The gentle no-sweat yoga people, most of whom are in their sixties or seventies, arrive at least fifteen minutes early and stand just outside the room, scowling at us through the plate-glass windows. My class is still going strong. We've got our weights, and the music's pumping, and we're working hard, sweating our heads off. We have a full ten minutes left, but one of them always pushes in and hollers over the music that it's time for us to wrap it up. She, for it is always a she, is furious for reasons so mysterious, I can't help but believe it's her habit to interact with the world in a high state of supreme grumpiness.

It's not always this way. Sometimes after class one of the

women will come up to me, touch my arm and say, "I just wanted to tell you that you girls are amazing!" We then trade a few words about how good it is to keep moving, and we wish each other well. But much of the time the gentle yoga people radiant a discontent so scorching, I feel a need to reapply sunscreen.

But I'm grateful for their presence, because it reminds me that the old saying about beauty being the light of the heart is not just a greeting card cliché. What makes these people "old" is their attitude, not how they look, and the reason I don't connect with them has nothing to do with their age, but with how they behave.

In Kaua'i, we have a neighbor down the road, Joe, a dapper man whose age could be anywhere between sixty and ninety. Every day he appears in his slacks and short-sleeved button-down shirt, his hair carefully combed. He's got shiny eyes, like a little elf. He cares for his lawn. He paints his own house. Everything in his realm is immaculate.

Joe allows himself a beer once a week, after he's mowed his lawn. One day we had some good Belgian beer in the house, and I brought him a bottle and asked him how it was going.

"Our friends have been here. For two weeks! That's a long time, especially since my wife's mind isn't so good, you know." I'd known for a while that Joe's wife had Alzheimer's. When I asked him how he was doing with that he said, "It teaches me over and over that acceptance is really a part of life."

Reece and Brody love Joe. Last year, when we returned to the neighborhood in the fall, he baked us a cake and delivered it with a big "Welcome back, Hamiltons!"

To thank Joe, Reece and Brody baked him a big cookie, and in return he wrote them a proper thank-you note. He tells them how proud he is of them. Brody adores him. Whenever he appears in front of his house she runs down the street and into his arms. I'm intrigued by this. There are a lot of other people in the neighborhood who are much younger, much hipper, and would seem to be much more fun from a four-year-old's point of view, and yet it's Joe—more specifically Joe's spirit—to which my four-year-old is drawn.

If an older person has that spirit, and all that life experience, is there anyone more badass? They're not running down the basketball court slam-dunking, but older people like Joe have a stillness and a wisdom and hopefully a sense of humor about life that you can *only* achieve by having lived that long.

I want to be like that.

I don't want to be the woman who's angry at the world because the clock keeps ticking.

There's a regular in my circuit training class who's fifty-eight. Beau is lithe and has the biceps of a thirty-year-old. She works hard and has a bright smile. She's spent a lot of time in the sun and the lines and freckles on her face reflect this. I don't know if she frets about her skin, but her vibrancy compensates for any imperfections. Watching Beau one day, I realized that, in the end, the only one who really cares about how we look is us. Does anyone care that I'm forty-two, or that I have this wrinkle here, or that tuck of cellulite there? Anyone?

Paradoxically, what people do tend to notice is how hard we're trying to look young. If we look as if we care too much, and if we spend a lot of time and money on procedures and hair appointments and spa treatments and trainers, that isn't appealing either. Most men hate it. Men tend to be intrigued by women who are happy, confident, and friendly. My very limited sampling includes Laird and some of his most accomplished pals, all of whom gravitate toward women who are self-possessed.

And who are these guys we're trying to look so young for? When I see a twenty-year-old, he doesn't appeal to me. I can recognize how handsome he might be, but my basic response is "What on earth would I do with *that*?" If trying to attract some youngster whom I'm not really interested in in any way is my sole reason for trying to look twenty-five, why bother? A young friend I used to play volleyball with took issue with this one day, pointing out that to be young and hot is to be wanted. But what about what *you* want? Being desired by someone else doesn't make us a better person, or even a more beautiful person. I learned this at a very young age, when I was living with my aunt Norette, who was warm, fun, and hilariously straightforward.

Once, when she'd taken me to Sears to buy some clothes, the saleswoman asked if I was her daughter. Norette is five feet tall, and at age seven, so was I. "Does she look like my daughter?" she snorted.

But she treated me as if I were. She loved me, was interested in what I was about as a person, and I loved her more than anyone. Norette was scrappy and overweight; she carried a good extra hundred pounds on her small frame, but I couldn't have cared less about her outward appearance.

Norette definitely influenced my attitude about aging: rather than try to be endlessly foxy, deep into middle age and beyond, my goal is to be handsome and distinguished and in command of my life. My goal is to be beloved; in the same way I love Aunt Norette, that's how I want the people in my life to feel about me.

That doesn't mean I don't fear getting older. On a basic existential level aging is scary. Philosophers spend their lives pondering the real terror associated with dying. I've heard it said that some people, when they're extremely old or extremely sick, might be ready to die. They might look at their lives and feel tired of the struggle. They might look at their middle-aged kids and think, "You know, I've heard that drama eight hundred more times than I really need to. I'm done."

But before that time, it's incredibly scary. It's a weakening of your body, yourself. You might feel wise and be able to seize the day better than you once did, but the bod is giving out. And the big question arises: Why is it that we live this life, we perform, we have a family, we get our kids out, and then we become so enfeebled? It's like having a beautiful dinner and eating a small piece of shit at the end.

The deterioration can be so humiliating. It's not as if one day you're bench-pressing a hundred and the next you're peeing in your pants in a movie theater. Usually it's gradual and devastating. Tiny terrors all along the way. Perhaps the ultimate lesson of getting older is learning to check our egos at the door. Still, when I see friends in the thrall of this process, it breaks me up. I don't want that for anyone. Losing our dignity and our independence is the fear beneath all the other anxiety about aging. It's not so much the lines and sunspots; it's more what the lines and sunspots signal: that life moves in only one direction.

Still, every day the sun rises, and each day is our own. I'm reminded of that Emerson quote, "No one suspects the days to be Gods." The one advantage of being older is knowing that our days truly are numbered. Every day we wake up and think, "I can be an asshole, or I can be badass."

STOP LOOKING SO HARD

Is there one modern American female who has not been trained to be hypercritical of her looks? Beginning at, oh, let's say age eleven, are not all of us taught to inspect, analyze, and criticize every inch of our bodies? How's our hair, skin, the length of our eyelashes, the shape of our butts, the size of our hips and breasts, and while we're at it, the perkiness of those breasts? Let's not forget our teeth or how white they are or the size of our lips. What if you have too much hair on your body? The checklist is endless.

The older we get, the less critical we should become about

our imperfections. At forty, we should be less critical than we are at thirty; when we're fifty, less critical still. Back off on your head-to-toe inspections. Stay away from the heinous magnifying mirror you come across in hotel bathrooms.

In the morning, or before you go out, just do a once-over.

Do I have my moments of weakness? Absolutely. All the time. I am human. But I try to have the discipline to resist, with every ounce of will I can muster, the urge to overexamine and criticize.

Some days I tell myself that in ten years I'll look back at how I am now and think how young and beautiful I was, and the thought of that makes me smile. None of us can escape the river of time, so let's float down it gracefully and happily.

As they say in Hawaii "Never mind." Which basically means let it go.

YOUR BODY REALLY IS A TEMPLE, EVEN IF IT'S AN OLD ONE

Just because you're older now than when you started reading this chapter, and just because there's nothing you can do, ultimately, but accept this as a natural part of human life, that doesn't mean you should resign yourself to living in nothing but elastic-waist jeans and oversized tees and prop yourself in front of the TV or computer, and order fries with that. It doesn't mean you should give up.

Michael Pollan, author of *The Omnivore's Dilemma*, has the best, easiest mantra for eating. "Eat food. Not too much. Mostly plants." I'd like to add: "break a sweat every day," "don't smoke," and "get sleep." You have to find the things that work for you. But the bottom line is that even if you're celebrating your ninety-eighth birthday, you should still take care of yourself.

Having a blueprint for self-care also ensures that you don't fall for every nonaging trend that comes down the pike. When one day you notice that butt line forming between your eyebrows you don't shriek and think, "It's time for a face-lift! A brow lift! Anything the plastic surgeon to the stars tells me to lift, I'm lifting!"

Once you reach a certain age, the big question on everyone's minds seems to be what is your official position on getting "work" done. People ask me about it all the time, and my response is that I don't know. Maybe I will, maybe I won't. If I'm still working I might like to freshen things up a bit one day, but I never want it to be a knee-jerk reaction.

ENJOY THE FLOWERS

Life is change, but one thing that never changes is that there's always a gaggle of beauties who are younger than you, hotter than you, and gaining the attention of the world in a way that you're unlikely to again, if you ever did in the first place. I'm not being negative; there are also people a hell of a lot older, more decrepit, and less fortunate than you.

I have three daughters, all of whom are blossoming flowers. I don't want to compete with them, or let their youth torture me. I want to enjoy watching them come into their own vibrant colors and celebrate all of their milestones. Here is the secret: I'm not in a race with them, or anyone for that matter. You can't be better or worse than anyone if you are not competing or comparing yourself to them. I know the torment of trying to race with someone. Try being in fashion surrounded by girls so beautiful they take your breath away. Or play a sport where some girls are so athletic and fluid their power just oozes out of every pore.

Bela has blossomed into a young woman, and even with Reece you can see that it's moments away. Intuitively, I've felt myself move to the side. But then, I've never wanted to be a person who was right in the middle anyway. That wasn't my thing. I didn't want the attention, even though because of my size I had it anyway. But I didn't seek it. I knew it wouldn't make *me* happy. Seeking attention for the sake of attention felt like trying to lure other people into giving me something, and I knew that wouldn't make me happy. What makes me happy? Do I feel good about the way I look? Am I comfortable in my clothes? Do I feel as if I'm representing who I really am?

AGE LIKE A GUY

Don Wildman founded Bally Total Fitness, but around our house he's known for his nine Ironman competitions, his devotion to heli-snowboarding, mountain biking, and stand-up paddling. If I haven't seen him around for a while, I assume he's in New York running a marathon or paddling the length of the Hawaiian Islands on a surfboard. Did I mention that

Don's seventy-nine? Laird, a mere forty-eight, trains with the Wild Man from time to time—a two-hour circuit that has been known to make professional athletes throw up. The most inspirational thing about Don is that, to him, his age is irrelevant. Sure, he eats an excellent diet—low in red meat, low in fat, high in plants—and takes supplements, including glucosamine for his increasingly creaky knees, but his main concern is the next adventure. His age doesn't keep him from doing one thing he wants to do.

I amuse myself imagining Don Wildman refusing to go to the beach because he thought he looked bad in a bathing suit, or Don Wildman skipping a day of snowboarding because the sun on the mountain that day was harsh and might cause more wrinkles or Don Wildman saying no to a mountain bike trip because he didn't want to look foolish because he wasn't a twenty-five-year-old hottie.

All that Don, or Laird, too, for that matter, care about is being able to do what they want to do. They don't think about their crow's-feet.

In this regard, I think women should aim to age as men do. To be brave enough to say, "Yeah, I have a wrinkle or two, what of it? That's who I am." I find it helpful to focus on what makes me genuinely happy, which then helps me project the kind of confidence that comes from feeling good about yourself. It helps me to remember that we are not only attracted to people because they are young and/or good-looking, but also because they are comfortable in their own skin, no matter their age.

8

IT'S ABOUT TIME

If there's anything good to be said about losing a parent when you're a child, it's that you learn the hard lesson early that time is precious. Right in front of your eyes there is the reality: a person really can be here one day and gone the next.

We all know this intellectually, yet we mismanage our time anyway. Some of us are superefficient, multitasking our heads off, filling our hours with chores, family demands, stuff that pops up on our screens, assuming that as long as we're "swamped" we're spending our time well. Then, when we do have down time, we're too discombobulated to use it wisely. How many times have I found myself with a blissful quiet hour to myself, that I then spend cruising for shoes online that I know I'm never going to buy?

DON'T KEEP YOUR PRIORITIES STRAIGHT

From day to day I try to get everything done I need to, then leave the door open for who knows what. Hey, let's go for a swim or a bike ride. Let's have a living room dance party.

Spontaneity is what makes life feel like an adventure, and we need a little of it every day.

We moms tend to get stuck on automatic pilot. "My family is my first priority," we say, without realizing this is actually a big-picture priority. Hour to hour, day to day, depending on what's going on, you really can put off the laundry or scheduling your kid's next playdate. On the day you're getting your appendix out, your health is the top priority, and the hubster and kids can make their own macaroni and cheese.

We need to know our priorities, but also that they aren't engraved on tablets like the Ten Commandments. We can change and rearrange them.

I imagine my priorities as existing on tiers, with the most important stuff on the top tiers. Fluffing the pillows? Probably (hopefully) bottom tier. Feeding the fam? Up near the top. But there are many other tiers, and given the day, they can be shuffled around according to what absolutely needs to get done.

Let's say it's a Monday, and you've had intimacy with your husband on Sunday; that could actually slide down to a lower tier. (Yes, even nookie has a tier.) But as the days pass, sex starts moving up until it's top-tier important.

If you trained on Monday and it's Tuesday, training could

be tucked onto a lower tier. If Tuesday's schedule is suddenly crazy because one of your kids got sick at school and had to be picked up, or the furnace went out and the repair guy's on his way, you can skip working out altogether. But the next day, Wednesday, training gets moved back up. For that day, it's a top-tier priority.

Having sex, working out, making the perfect dinner, scrubbing the bathrooms spotless—not killer important every day. If you had an awesome, multicourse dinner last night, maybe tonight it's a one-pot dinner. Or Chinese takeout. If the kids have four activities Thursday, it's okay to bum around Friday.

Take care of the top-tier items, then do something for yourself. Read a book, work on your knitting, call somebody up and go for a walk. We need to get over the idea that if we have a free hour between, say, 2:30 and 3:30 that we need to jam it with chores or compulsive emailing. You don't have to know all this seven months in advance. At the beginning of the day you can make some executive decisions about what you need to pay attention to and what you can let ride.

Once you move something down to the bottom tier, stop worrying about it. Don't let it nag at you. Most of all, don't beat up on yourself.

JUST TO-DO IT

People get hysterical about being organized, but really, you just need a list and you need to check off the items, starting at the top. It's as simple as that. The power of the list is that it's there in black and white, and you can run a line through an item. Done!

Without a list it's too easy to plunge into mom mania, where you run around in circles with a spatula in one hand and a soccer cleat in the other, freaking out because you have so much to do, somuchtodo, *somuchtodo*!!!!!!

Getting swept up in freak-outs over little things does nothing but contribute to the great flood of toxic emotion. And it's only worse when we're sleep deprived or our schedules are too jam-packed. Decorating cupcakes for a party can seem as important as stopping the flow of blood from a head wound.

The bad thing about feeling overwhelmed is that it's not just counterproductive, it's also destructive. Once we're overwhelmed, it's easy to decide that rather than tackling all the things we need to do, we would rather sit down on the couch with a bag of chips. An hour later, we're no closer to getting our chores done, plus we feel queasy from the junk food and, worse, full of self-loathing.

You don't need a special device to make a to-do list. You don't even need a notebook. I feel somewhat ridiculous saying this, but you'd be surprised how many people say they can't get organized until they take a workshop or hire an organizer or get the proper datebook. The back of an envelope will do. And the best thing about it? When you're done, you can get rid of it.

THE JOY OF OUTSIDE

After our work is done for the day and we've more or less tackled our to-do list, how do we spend the rest of our hours? In the same way we need to know our priorities, we need to have a sense of what kind of activities are fun and spontaneous. For me, it's being in nature, being with friends, and community service. Pretty much everything else is off my radar completely. You'll never catch me shopping until I drop, cooking a complicated French meal, or jamming with an all-girl band.

Fifteen years ago, Laird and I bought a piece of hilly property overlooking the Hanalei River. Kaua'i is called the Garden Island, but what that really means is the jungle island. The view from our as-yet-to-be-built house will look west over the canopy of banana, banyan, and palms to the elongated S of the Hanalei that winds to the sea, the jagged mountains of the Hono'onapali Reserve, and, beyond that, the unworldly cloud-enshrouded peaks of the Na Pali Coast. It's a study in shades of green, blue, and pale gray. It's Bali Ha'i.

There are plenty of perfectly good houses in Kaua'i, but we wanted one that was plain and comfortable and allowed us to live our daily lives in a way that we could never, for a minute, forget about the natural world unfolding around us.

At Florida State, I spent a lot of time on indoor courts. When I began modeling, around the same time, I spent half the year in New York City. I sometimes wonder how my life would have gone had I hooked up with someone I'd met in Manhattan, a photographer, say, or magazine editor, some indoor person. One of the major things that attracted me to Laird was his abiding relationship with nature.

Even back then I could feel it. The more time I spent in a fancy dress and proper shoes, the further away I felt from who I truly was. There is a lot of talk today about how our children are suffering a nature deficit, how computer screens have become their reality and forests, meadows, creeks—even a nearby empty lot where weeds and wildflowers grow—something foreign, something "other."

It's true for adults, too. It's true for you. When was the last time you looked up from your device and noticed the wind blowing through the trees?

We're always looking for complicated answers to our complicated problems. Do we need to buy something new? See a new kind of counselor? Find a new partner? Move to a new state or country? Do we need to completely overhaul our bad habits? Indulge in retail therapy?

There are no guarantees in this book. My foot is too big for the glass slipper. I'm not a believer in easy fixes or fairy tales. Except when it comes to this: put down your book or eReader and go take a walk around the block. You don't even need to live on a beautiful block, with carefully tended gardens or towering trees. You don't need a view. Just be out there. Inhale. Crane your neck up at the sky. Notice the weather. Whatever is going on in your life, it'll get better. Even if the only thing that improves is your outlook.

LOG OFF, GET HAPPY

Some wise man said, "The dose makes the poison." The Internet is a little bit like that, most of us rely on it for work, for our social lives, for our entertainment, but too much is toxic.

Yes, it's nice to be able to read the paper online, and could there be anything more wonderful, at the end of a long day, than Huluing a few episodes of *The Daily Show*? But do you know a single soul who leaves it at that? Do you know anyone who says, "Hm, I don't remember who was president before Woodrow Wilson," or asks, "Which has more vitamin C, rasp-berries or strawberries?" then looks it up and immediately logs off? Anyone?(Well, Laird does. Every once in a while he wants to see what kind of sails they're manufacturing in Sweden or something. He checks it out, and five minutes later the computer is off. But he's probably the only person in America.)

I don't know what percentage of time well-intentioned googling leads down the rabbit hole of checking out celebrity baby bumps; looking up the five (eight or thirteen) dumbest criminals ever; the latest on Justin Bieber's hair; six ways you're shaving your legs wrong; cute kitties, puppies, baby dolphins; or finding out which celebrity is in jail again.

One click leads to another leads to feeling like shit about your life. Whether it's the latest expert on mommying who has scientific evidence that however you're raising your kids is wrong, or the old high school friend who pops up on Facebook with a better ass than yours, which is documented in the ninety-two photos of her annual vacation in Tuscany. Before you know it, you've clicked through to every single shot, and you've wasted twenty minutes in pathetic voyeurism you'd never allow yourself to lapse into in real life. It's like the whole wide world of the web has been engineered to make you feel bad about yourself.

We must unplug. Forget taking pictures of your Jamaican vacation, just live the thing. Just live your life in the moment.

If you were stuck sitting next to someone on an airplane who spewed at you the kind of stuff you surf online, you'd think you'd entered a level of Dante's hell. You'd be telling friends about the bore you got stuck next to on your flight to Atlanta. A few years ago the idea of watching slides of someone's vacation to Greece was only marginally more appealing than a tax audit; now, bizarrely, it's become gripping.

I'm willing to admit I may be more sensitive to this than most people. When I Google myself—and I have, exactly once—it made me queasy. Even though there's a lot of positive, of course my eye was drawn to the nasty stuff.

"When did Gabrielle Reece start looking like a man?"

"I never realized Gabrielle Reece was so giant."

My friend sent me a link to a foot fetish site. I have big feet, and there they are. Bigger than life. And there are comments. People going back and forth about my feet. So I turned it off. I don't need my mind poisoned by that shit.

Laird knows and cares even less about what's going on online than I do. He doesn't know, he doesn't look, he doesn't care. He simply doesn't. And I think he's happier for it. Every once in a while someone will write him something profound and heavy, and then I'll force him to listen while I read it to him, but even then, it doesn't really register. He doesn't really care who thinks he's da man. He's equipped with a strong internal anchor, and he just doesn't get swept away.

Aside from time-wasting, mind-mushing, and depression-inducing, too much time online moves you even further away from your body, and from the natural world. It moves you further up into your head.

I'm curious to see how my children are going to manage it, in their lives and in their relationships. It's going to be a challenge for them to stay in touch with themselves, with their beliefs and their feelings in a world where there are no more Sundays, no more silent three o'clock in the mornings. I'm praying for a backlash, for a bunch of kids in Oregon to take up the cause of letter writing and turn it into a global movement.

THE SECRET WEAPON FOR DAYS THAT SUCK

Some days just suck. This is true for everyone—overworked moms included. Some days all I do is wrangle everyone. I make sure the kids get where they need to get on time. I make sure Laird's business chores get seen to. Some days, I'm simply the least fun person you've ever met.

I remind myself that it's only *one* day. Also, that this wrangling is part of the thing I signed up for. I'm in the trenches, and I try to embrace my duties, even when they're mind-numbing or maddening. Then the question becomes, given how this day's gone to hell, how can I make the best of it?

The thing that can turn that kind of day around for me?

Helping a sister out.

If time permits, and I see that one of my girlfriends is slammed, I'll volunteer to take one of her kids from here to there. If I can make her life even a little better by doing some extra chauffeuring, I'm there. Doing a favor for a friend can make me feel good about what I've signed up for.

I have friends to whom I say "I'll take your kids for the afternoon" and they say "Oh no, I don't want you to go out of your way." But I don't put myself in positions I don't want to be in very often; I don't have time to do things just to be nice.

And neither do you.

Women tend to be overly concerned with everyone else's happiness. I've noticed a habit among some chicks I know: they automatically say "yes" to everything because they imagine it's easier. Will you make some cookies for the party? Yes! Chair the PTA fund-raiser? Of course! Host a dinner party for sixteen of Mr. Charming's most important business associates? Not a problem! It's not as if they *want* to say no; they just don't know *what* they want to say. They don't take the time to know what they want.

My friends and I are not scorekeepers. If it's convenient for them to take my kids to a pool party, then they do, and not just because I had their kids the week before. It really does take a village, and I want my village populated with authentic, self-governing women who are strong, generous, and nurturing, and who feel free to say no to me when they can't help, but they're quick to say yes when they can.

In Kaua'i, I have a friend named Caridyn who grew up with Laird and whose husband, Coppin, is my volleyball husband. Every Saturday, for the six months the family is based in Kaua'i, Coppin and I team up and play on the beach with the rest of the boys.

Caridyn is one of those women whose charisma is rooted in her sense of self; she likes her life and who she is in it. On any given day, Caridyn will cook you a meal while tending to her four daughters, and still manage to get out in the morning to catch the surf.

I have a different way about me. I'm not an ice queen, but it's a different style. I believe my kids feel a great deal of security with me. They know that mom's right there. And I'm consistent. I don't change much from day to day. I make their breakfast, lunch, and dinner every day. They know they're safe with me. I'm there to listen. When Reece wants to talk to me I can listen without having to jump in and "parent." I take care of everybody, but it's not all warm and fuzzy Italian mama. I'm matter-of-fact and direct. Sometimes it's been hard, but it's the only way I can do it.

The nurturing part for me hasn't come easily. I learn from

the women around me. I try to keep myself surrounded with people who share my priorities, but who handle life in different ways, people I can learn from.

If I find myself getting caught up in the taxing minutiae of a legitimately shitty day, I can call Caridyn. It's important to have those kinds of people in your life. We all need to cultivate relationships with individuals who can enlarge our perspectives and calm our nerves just by being who they are.

EVERY MINUTE OF EVERY DAY YOU'RE WRITING THE STORY OF YOUR LIFE

Sometimes I think this lack of time is a problem we invent for ourselves.

I don't know whether we work ourselves into an eye twitch and a marriage counselor because it makes us feel virtuous, or because we believe somehow that if every night we collapse from exhaustion the universe will reward us with happy, productive children and a husband who sticks around. Maybe it's because we're afraid that if we have any spare time, we'll be pressed into experiencing the burden of figuring out what to do with it. As long as you're running around hysterically, taking care of everything that crosses your path, you'll never have to figure out what you want, or what makes you happy.

I know, kids take up a lot of time. No one knows that better than I do.

But what if you had an hour a day that belonged only to you? A day, a week a month? What would you do with it?

Our friend Paul Chek, who works with top professional athletes, movie stars, and billionaires, told me something I've never forgotten. His clients are people who have what everyone wants, they are at the pinnacle of their careers, and by every measurement they've achieved success. And yet many of them are unhappy. The thing that slayed me was this: when Paul tried to find out what would make them happy, if they could have anything or change anything in their lives, they had no idea.

My happiness is tied directly to my sense of peace. For me, it's about keeping it simple. I try not to overcomplicate my life, and I try to remain a pretty fierce steward of my time. I'm always aware how whatever I do serves me. Which is why I commit a certain number of hours a month to community service.

Laird and I serve on the board of Rain Catchers, whose mission is to provide clean water to people in every corner of the globe. We also work with Heal the Bay, a local organization dedicated to protecting and restoring our beautiful local Santa Monica Bay, and the National Resources Defense Council, devoted to protecting wildlife and the wild places of the world.

Mostly, we donate training or surfing sessions to raise money for charities we support. If it's in the wheelhouse of nature or children, we're in. The most fun is getting to work with a gang of kids. My friend Kelly Meyer created

Teaching Gardens, aimed at teaching kids from first grade to fifth the basics of gardening and the joy of eating what you grow. I usually parachute in for a short session on movement.

I can see your thought bubble from here: "Isn't community service a sentence handed down by a judge?"

Think of it this way: service serves you as much as it does whomever you're trying to help. Aside from the obvious and immediate good feeling it bestows, it offers some perspective on your issues. It helps you stand back and appreciate your life. How's the fam? Pretty good. Hubster? Yep. Job? Could use another, but at least I have one.

It's also a good message to send our kids who generally watch what we *do* more closely than they listen to what we *say*. Spending part of your time on a service project is inconvenient and there's no monetary gain. You're doing it because you want to contribute to the betterment of your world, which, by the way, conveys to your kids that they're not the center of the known universe. Could there be a better message for them?

If we never take the time to get out of our bubble and interact with people outside our normal sphere, we risk becoming hypochondriacs of our own lives. We fall into overexamining every glance our husband throws us, the mild rash on the inside of our kid's elbow, the new wrinkle beside our eye—wait, that is a wrinkle, isn't it? Or do I need glasses, oh shit, I need glasses! It can be endless if you let it be endless.

But it doesn't have to be that way. And I've found that you can reconnect with what's really crucial versus what's noise-in garbage by going outside your bubble and helping others. No one said it better than Gandhi: "The best way to find yourself is to lose yourself in the service of others."

9

KEEPING THE HAPPILY IN THE EVER AFTER

Last year there was a poll asking women what they'd give up in order to have a beach-perfect body. The consensus was 67 percent would give up sex for six months. Or maybe it was 78 percent would give up sex for four months. And 83 percent said they would give up sex for two months? Really, the thing was so stupid I didn't even finish reading the article. The takeaway is that we chicks value being admired and envied over intimacy.

Heads up, modern women: men don't care if you have a half-inch of muffin top perched on the waistband of your jeans, or a smidge of cellulite beneath your left butt cheek. They don't care if, when you twist around, there's a little wedge of fat in the lower midriff region. They don't care if, when you raise your arm, there's a teeny wobble beneath your triceps. Do not care.

All they want is for you, their chick, to be naked and smiling.

And if you want your partnership to last, you better plan on being naked and smiling. A lot.

Most days, the sporting event my marriage most resembles is the four-hundred-meter relay, where the only time you have any contact with your teammate is when he passes off the baton, and for about thirty feet you're running side by side before he falls away and you zoom off.

All last week Laird was shooting something for French TV. The French are mesmerized by Laird and the way he lives and they were shooting something lifestyle-y, but I wasn't sure what, exactly. He was gone before the sun rose and home long after the girls were put to bed. I was teaching all week and also participated in a volleyball tournament, and the girls each had their full complement of ballet, gymnastic, jujitsu, and horseback riding lessons. Someone may have had an ear infection in there, too.

We were both exhausted, and you know what happens when you're exhausted? What is the very first thing women take a pass on?

Exactly.

Why it's more important to make sure the four-year-old's tiny T-shirts are folded into tiny squares and tucked into her drawer in a tidy stack than to be intimate with Mr. Charming is an excellent question. I'm sure it has to do with the feeling of satisfaction we gain—all right, *I* gain—from checking something off my to-do list.

Laird and I can go on like this for, oh, about forty-eight hours, after which Mr. Charming's behavior toward me starts to change. My girlfriends are convinced that, after a few days, if the guys don't receive the right kind of attention, they start treating us like they treat everyone else in the household.

And you know who that is in my household? A teenager who's never there, two little kids, and Mr. Speedy, the dog. And Mr. Charming, who, once he's gone without for three days, starts getting grumpy. The word "withdrawal" comes to mind.

I might be traveling, might be doing the taxes, or the kids might be sick. It doesn't really matter. Forty-eight hours passes and I better start thinking about some naked and smiling time. So doing Laird is on my to-do list.

We're interluders, grabbing time when the kids are off somewhere in the middle of the day. We're big on nap dates. Even if he's cruised through the kitchen and I say, "Hey, what are you doing in half an hour," and he's busy, it's good for him to know I'm thinking about him. And it.

And yes, even though he's the one who's got the forty-eight-hour withdrawal problem, I'm the one chasing him around the sofa. We women complain about this perceived unfairness. Why do we have to do everything (and pretty much every woman I know does *everything*, defined, for our purposes, as more than one person can possibly handle in a day, week, month, lifetime), and then, at the end of the day, find a way to channel our inner pole dancer?

Because once women get all snuggled down into a relationship, sex just isn't the priority it once was. I wish I could report otherwise. But the sun rises and sets; it's the end of the day and we're dead tired. We're not withholding, we're not bored with our partners (unless we are, but that's another issue), we really are simply exhausted. And the more exhausted we are, the more days pass without sex—for some couples there's more sexiness at a sixth grader's slumber party, where at least the boys next door might get in on some spin the bottle action, than there is five, six, seven years into a marriage.

It's important for Mr. Charming to know that we still think of him that way. Also, unless he has a wasting disease, Mr. Charming will pretty much drop everything and have sex whenever you let it be known that you're up for it (down with it?), and there are few things less erotic, not to mention humiliating, than for your guy to sidle up to you and nibble on your earlobe only to have you bat him away and say, "Sorry, babe, the PTA cupcake committee is meeting in fifteen minutes, then I have to stop by and pick up some new fly strips for the garage."

I had a boyfriend in my twenties, a sincere and generous guy whom I knew from the modeling world. He was very understanding about my time, my work schedule, my training schedule, my moods. Too understanding, as it turns out. One day we just stopped having sex altogether, and once we stopped, I lost all interest. He was a great guy—and by the way, this was a beautiful man—but I didn't want to sleep with him. Once it got to the point where he had to ask "Are you not attracted to me?" the relationship was over.

With Laird, it's different. He has expectations that if he's committed to the relationship, I'm committed to an active sex life. He lets me know on a regular basis that he's *here*, and because he has high expectations on the sex front, I rise to meet those expectations. It's not as if it's difficult. It isn't as if he's off scratching himself and honking at me, "Okay, woman, come over here and boff my brains out." Laird is a loving guy who pays attention to me.

So yeah, bottom line: if you want everything to run smoothly in the castle, get busy. Sex takes, what, twenty minutes? You should never *have* to fake it, but you know what? You're not going to go to intimacy hell if once in a while you fake it. And if you have to indulge in a fantasy, do it. Sometimes I imagine Laird with another woman. I look at it from the outside, as is my habit, and I think, "Whoa! That guy's attractive. He's hot!" Do whatever it takes to remind you of what you have. And, presumably, what you want to keep.

And while we're on the subject of what you might need to tell yourself from time to time to get into the spirit of the occasion, how about checking in with your guy to see if he's still digging the way you're stroking, sucking, or tugging? If you ask him how he likes his lamb chop, there's no reason you shouldn't ask him about his more intimate preferences. Time changes things for them, too. Ten years ago a little tug of the balls might have been just the surprise that ramped up the intensity; now, it's merely annoying. We talk a lot about being productive in the gym, why not in the bedroom as well? Also, nothing says "I care" like letting Mr. Charming know you're thinking about sex with him.

If you do take the time—let's go crazy and say forty-five minutes from kicking off your shoes to zipping up your jeans—to nourish that part of your marriage, it's also one less thing to feel bad about.

Once, a friend pointed out that sometimes we take a pass on sex not because we're exhausted or not interested in our partners, but because we're not feeling sexy ourselves. We've had a crap day and we're bloated and broken out; whatever our private version of hot is, we're the opposite.

But guess what? Men see only what we project.

In the same way the basket of unfolded laundry in the middle of the living room is completely invisible to them when they're watching the play-offs, so, too, do they fail to see any of your flaws when you're giving them the hungry-for-love look. At that moment, they are completely oblivious to your need to exfoliate, trust me.

But if you beg off sex saying that it's because you feel fat or your knees are too scaly or your forearm skin is too crepey or you have a zit on your chin, you've basically created a big red neon arrow that points to something he would have never even noticed.

Here's an experiment: the next time you're feeling too bad about your body to initiate sex, do it anyway. Grab your guy and be like, "Hey, I'm so hot right now and you're going to get lucky." If he says, "Um, no, sorry, your thighs look a little big today, not interested," it will be such as astonishing example of human male behavior, you should write your own book. More likely, you're going to make his week. He's thinking, "Wow, my chick's in a great mood. She's happy and she wants me."

The person in your head analyzing every inch of your physical being is not a man, but a woman. She's evaluating how you walk, what your backside looks like, how smooth your skin is, and whether anyone can tell how cheap your handbag is. And if the woman in your head is keeping you from the happily in the ever after, you've got to shut her up.

I've spent most of my life around male athletes. Regardless of their sport, they all have this in common: they're all walking, talking testosterone factories traveling the world, where women offer themselves up any time they stop for more than ninety seconds. And it's not just the jocks; corporate guys are often on the road two hundred fifty days a year, meeting a variety of interesting, dynamic women. Available women. Even the guy who lives a relatively quiet life nevertheless comes into contact with hot baristas every day, or the new intern at the office.

I'm not trying to make you paranoid; I just want to point

out that there's opportunity for men pretty much everywhere, and if they're not committed to their partners or their relationships, which is more liable to happen if they're being neglected, the more likely they are to succumb to their hardwiring, which is to cast the net wide.

So often a guy meets someone else and the woman sings this sad song: "I was left for a younger woman, woe is me." But that's not why she was left. In a lot of instances, she was left because she stopped paying attention.

If we're only mothers, if we're only dutiful wives, if the man to whom we were once head-over-heels attracted gets sidelined, then ignored, that's a problem.

PRAISE THE LORD

People need praise. Just think how good it makes you feel when your guy compliments you on, oh, pick anything: your new dress, jambalaya recipe, masterful downward-facing dog, ability to solve for x. However good that makes you feel, multiply that by ten and you have the degree to how happy your guy feels when you compliment him.

Men need praise, and they need it from women. From the time they're learning to ride their first bike and saying "Look, Ma, no hands!" (notice: the old saying isn't "Look, Dad, no hands), for men, the world is a better place when they are getting their egos stroked a little by the women in their lives. They're fragile beings, men. Fragile, but also powerful. Sometimes I think of them as racehorses, huge and majestic, but also capable of breaking down in an instant. Even the most successful man, surrounded by people in his professional life telling him he's so smart or so talented, still needs his partner to tell him I love you, I appreciate you, I desire you—and he needs to hear it on a regular basis.

I wonder if, reading this, you're rolling your eyes, thinking, "Wait, I work fifty hours a week, do the laundry, shopping, cooking, and pick his dirty boxers up off the bathroom floor every morning, *and* I'm supposed to praise him for the masterful way in which he changed the oil in the car, or made pancakes last Sunday morning, or can pick out 'Hotel California' on the guitar?"

Yep.

It helps to have some basic human empathy. "Be kind, for everyone you meet is fighting a great battle" was the advice Plato gave to his buddies, and it's just as true today. For example, do we women know what it's like for a guy to feel as if he's not a young buck anymore? We're so quick to say, "Oh, he's having a midlife crisis" when he goes out and buys that little red sports car, but what does that really mean? How is it that we women are allowed to talk (read: obsess) about our fears of aging and yet we assume for them it's a big joke?

Even the most gentle, mild-mannered men thrive when they get a little appreciation. When I was a kid and living with my aunt and uncle, my uncle Joe never said much. He was a soft-spoken guy, tired from his long days at work. He and

Aunt Norette scrimped and saved, and after many years of sticking to their budget, he was able to purchase a twenty-four-foot sailboat. He loved that boat like a family member. And every once in a while Norette would get him talking about sailing, and even though I was a tiny child, I could see new shades of his personality I'd never seen before. Whatever the man version of blossoming is, that's what my uncle Joe was doing beneath the glow of Aunt Norette's interest and empathy.

There's that famous, droll Virginia Woolf quote about how women were trained to act as mirrors, reflecting men back at twice their normal size. It would be easy to smirk if they didn't benefit from it so much.

IT'S A DISAGREEMENT, NOT A DUEL TO THE DEATH

One of the basic agreements a couple makes is who's the male and who's the female. It usually breaks down along obvious gender lines, but not always. And the point isn't who's the one who strides out of the house at seven a.m. with a briefcase and who takes the babies to play group, it's the agreement you make when you commit.

I wish this was my own clever idea, but it's part of the wisdom according to Dr. Patricia Allen, an L.A.-based cognitive behavioral therapist and expert on communication in relationships. She's got a big cult following, and several best-selling books, including *Getting to "I Do": The Secret to Doing*

Relationships Right and her most recent, written with Don Schmincke, *The Truth About Men Will Set You Free . . . but First It'll P*** You Off.*

Dr. Pat Allen (like a superhero, she's known to one and all as Dr. Pat Allen; her children probably call her Dr. Pat Allen) says that when you get married, its key that both parties understand that one of two things is happening: either you're providing the female energy and Mr. Charming is providing the male, or you're assuming the male role and he, the female. In a long-term relationship the roles may switch. Men, as they get older and their testosterone levels drop, tend to get all nesty and interested in snuggling and watching a movie; women, on the other hand, once the nest is empty and their estrogen is in retreat, are like, "I'm off to raft the Grand Canyon. See ya."

This role reversal often happens gradually over time. That's natural. But one important thing to remember is that you should never flip the switch on your understanding with your partner, especially not during the middle of an all-out fight. The people responsible for wedding vows in the *Book of Common Prayer* should tuck that in somewhere: that we vow not to pull the rug out from under the other guy by switching gender roles in the middle of a spat. If you've agreed in calmer moments that you're going to provide the male energy, you can't suddenly flip out and say, "I can't take supporting your ass anymore! Get a job or I'm outta here." Or, if you're rocking the female energy, you can't throw a plate of spaghetti at Mr. Charming's head and scream, "I'm tired of cooking and cleaning and taking care of the kids! I'm going back to get my MBA!"

The masculine-feminine dynamic is more complicated than it might seem on the face of it. To be truly feminine means being soft, receptive, and—look out, here it comes—submissive. My own level of submission and commitment to Laird became greater when I had my kids. I've bowed down to this family on every level I can. That said, to run a household you've got to be a badass. I keep myself from going insane by this paradox by pretending I'm in a nature documentary about, say, wild mustangs, where you've got the lead mare who brooks no shit and keeps everyone in line, including the stallions, and the lower subset females, who are sweet and cooperative and go along to get along. I'm one or the other, moment to moment.

Laird and I argue. The disagreements are genuine, but they're on a sliding scale of importance.

One of our ongoing arguments is whether to get Mr. Speedy neutered. Every time I take Mr. Speedy to the vet, I get a lecture. Laird adores Mr. Speedy, and worries that if he gets his balls lopped off Mr. Speedy will become Mr. Slow Poke. It's become a huge nuisance; everyone in the neighborhood takes a dim view of Mr. Speedy wandering the streets humping everything in sight. But Laird stands firm. Once, when he was away, I thought about just getting the dog fixed, but now Reece and Brody have taken up the cause. "No!" they cry. "That's Dad's dog. You can't get rid of his balls!" (And now, balls have become a huge topic in our house. Once, someone told four-year-old Brody that the softest part of a horse was his nose, and she retorted, "No, it's his balls.")

The more serious arguments revolve about his (infrequent) criticism of the way I organize his business matters. Recently, in putting together our new website, we shot three thousand (yes, thousand) pictures of Laird and I doing individual workouts for men and women. The photographer was disorganized and the whole thing wound up being a lot more effort than we'd anticipated. When I groused about it he said, "Well, you know, the decision to hire him started at the top."

"I take full responsibility for hiring him," I said.

"You asked me what I thought and I told you it was a bad idea," he said.

"No, actually, I didn't ask your opinion at all," I said.

A friend said her husband has a rule, and it's a good one: "You can tell me what to do, or you can tell me how to do it, but you can't do both." That's pretty much how I was feeling at that exact moment. I got in the shower, and Laird followed me in.

"Hey, let me fume a little," I said. And he backed off.

Usually we fight when we're tired, overworked, and frustrated.

When an argument is over, it's over. Once he's apologized and you've accepted it, or you've apologized and he's accepted it, guess what? It's done. By accepting the apology you're saying you've also agreed to move on, and not belabor the issue a second longer.

If you're not ready to do this, if you feel like you need another seven minutes (or seven hours or seven days) of re-hash, then *say so*. It's completely permissible to say, "I'm sure I'll forgive you before the end of the next Ice Age, but it's not going to be today."

KICKING CHARMING TO THE CURB

But all of this—the dedication to keeping sex alive, taking daily opportunities to give your guy some props, cultivating empathy for what it's like for him in your marriage and in the world, and making an effort to fight fair—is only in play when your partner is committed to the relationship.

What do I mean by this? It's not simply being under the same roof sucking up the same air and eating your mac 'n' cheese.

I had a friend who'd gotten married pretty young. She had a great guy. Smart, funny, cool. If she needed the tire replaced on her car, it was done the next day. What he never got was that part of his husband job was also to take a little time to ask my friend how her day was, or to stop and tell her she looked pretty that day. Weirdly, he never asked what she'd done that day, or even where she'd been. They got along, but there was this place where they didn't intersect.

It's not as if we need to be monitored, we don't need a chip implanted in our asses, but we do need to feel as if our guy is keeping an eye on us, is watching out for us. Mr. Charming, if he is to be truly charming, needs to know when to step it up on this front, to realize that you're not his drinking buddy, his mom, his sister, or his daughter. You're his queen. And you need to be treated that way. This isn't chivalry, exactly. It's more like when you mist a flower and it perks right up.

Laird is as good at showing me this type of attention as he is at surfing, but I'll tell you this: if, in a few years' time, it was all me, all the time, with the Shiny Eyes and the Interludes and the compliments, and I'd made sure I'd communicated my thoughts and feelings on his lack of commitment and got no response, I would seriously reevaluate.

A WORD ON CHEATING

If you've got a guy who's out there actively screwing around, who's more interested in succumbing to his hardwiring than in making an effort to be in a relationship with you, then don't bother. It's time to move on.

Most men think it's their own gender out there shaking the trees for someone new, but women can truly excel at being unfaithful. Our reasons for doing it are generally varied and complicated. Most of us aren't "Ooh! I'd love to tap that," which is pretty much the beginning and the end of the male impulse. Women step out for a number of reasons: the need for companionship, intimacy, tenderness, affection. Some-times we're throwing down a gauntlet. Show me the chick who has to tell the back of her video-game addicted husband's head she's unhappy two dozen times, and I'll show you the chick who gets it going with the pool boy.

Men are straightforward. Their wives aren't putting out, so they sneak in a nooner with the temp. But women are devious. We're better liars and better manipulators and just all around better cheaters. It's amazing to me that the CIA isn't completely comprised of females. We're shifty and, when we get to the land of cheating, ruthless.

Oh dear husband, you tool, I have cheated on you, and not only have I cheated on you, but see that toothbrush you're brushing your teeth with right this very minute? He brushed his teeth with it only hours ago.

A guy would never do that.

But let me tell you: no good ever comes from it. If you're going to go down that road, you might as well just have the courage to leave. If your Self on Monday, who hasn't yet had the interlude with the pool boy, could have a conversation with your Self on Wednesday, after it's happened, she would probably say, "Don't do it. Not worth it."

But for some reason those two Selves never seem to talk.

The worst of it is not that you've betrayed someone to whom you've made a promise, but that you've broken your own code; most of us don't aspire to cheat, be devious, or betray. And we don't feel good about ourselves after we've done those things.

All this said, I do believe in the value of a Get Out of Jail Free card, especially if we're talking a one-night stand and it's not connected to a web of dishonesty.

You've got to trust your instincts to tell the difference. If you have the sense that your guy is keeping a lot of his life hidden, there's some dishonesty there. If he spends a lot of time away from you that's unaccounted for, or spends a lot of time going out with the guys and getting toasted, or if he quickly closes his computer when you enter the room, or takes his phone into the bathroom with him (to text in secret or to prevent you from seeing his texts), something's up, something he's keeping from you. You're no longer sharing a life.

But if the foundation is solid and the relationship is good, you really can forgive, forget, and move on. Life is long and often complex, and humans are, by their nature, deeply flawed.

And we're not princesses, after all.

10

DON'T GET IMPALED ON THE WHITE PICKET FENCE

Not long ago I read a magazine story entitled something like "I love my kids and hate my life." It was about how, despite how much we love our children, and how empty and loveless our lives would be without them, we parents are basically miserable. Mothers are less happy than fathers, and the more children you have, the less happy you are. The author wasn't talking about joy, about the mystery and miracle of unconditional parental love, but about how day-to-day life sucks when you've got kids underfoot.

The piece went on to talk about how part of the misery might be a result of all the hyperparenting going on, the over-the-top ambition middle- and upper-middle-class parents have for their children, and the sheer daily horror of being in the car so much, "Driving Miss Daisy" as a friend calls it, shuttling kids hither and yon for hours on end, all day long.

True confessions: I'm a little amused by all this outrage.

What did people *think* having a family was going to be like?

My four-year-old can tell you that the commercials are make-believe, why do adults seem to have trouble with this concept?

LOWER YOUR EXPECTATIONS, SERIOUSLY

Buying into the white-picket-fence scam begins at the wedding. No, I take that back: any single chick who's out there planning her wedding before she's even met the guy is setting herself up for a big reality smack up the side of the head.

Somewhere along the way the wedding ceremony has morphed from a man and a woman celebrating their union in front of family and friends, to a celebration of the bride's need to be princess for a day. The focus is no longer even on the couple; it's a day of lavish overspending so that the chick will feel magical, so she will feel as if her life as a boring single person who lives on premade food from Trader Joe's and watches five hours of *Law & Order* reruns on a Saturday night is about to end, and she's going to be a Mrs., starring in her own edition of the West Elm catalog.

This never happens. There are books and television shows

and movies galore that are being released into the culture every seventy-two hours that refute this version of matrimony; there are cousins and college roommates and high school best friends who get drunk on occasion and spill the beans about the reality of married life; there is the divorce rate, which hovers just under fifty percent and has for forty years.

And still, the myth of the white picket fence remains.

The best thing that can happen to a couple is that on their wedding night, she throws up and he stinks up the bathroom with his man farts. Instantly, they become real to each other.

So, one way to avoid having your completely unrealistic expectations dashed to smithereens is to attempt to understand what you're getting into. Keep your head on straight. When it comes to the wedding, never lose sight of the fact that going into debt for what is basically just a party isn't worth it. Even if it means you get to wear a tiara. Not worth it. Just ask MasterCard. They don't care if you were a princess for a day, they're still charging eighteen percent interest. When it comes to Mr. Charming, remember last summer when his allergies were in full bloom, and he flung himself on the sofa for a week and watched all of the Star Wars films, and sneezed and moaned and his mother came to visit and made his favorite cobbler and rubbed his feet and whispered about you behind your back? That is what you've married.

That "for better and for worse" part in the vows? It's real.

Which doesn't mean there isn't a lot of deep happiness and life-changing awesomeness. There is. But there's a lot of crap, too. Even behind the white picket fence.

DEALING WITH THE WHAT IS

I'm a gig-mom, a hybrid of the working mom and the stay-at-home mom. My career has ramped down since I've had my kids, but I continue to do the occasional gig, appearance, lecture, magazine cover, training class, and fitness workshop.

Recently, I did a lecture and the group hosting it said they didn't care what I said, so long as I didn't get into the Mommy War mess. Even though they insisted that I remain authentic and honest and speak my mind, they didn't want me to speak my mind about *that*.

It's a hot-button issue because all of us, wherever and whoever we are, suspect we're supposed to be doing something else. When life is particularly challenging, we feel this most strongly. When our kids seem too needy and we're too broke to purchase new tires for the car and it feels as if we haven't gotten out of our yoga pants in six months, and our marketing director sister-in-law, with skin that looks newly facialized and a handbag that costs a month's mortgage, enthuses about her new project at work, we think we're idiots for not having a quote unquote real job. Conversely, when we're hammered at work and eating crap microwave burritos at our desk and we rush home to see our kids, who sob when the babysitter leaves, and we try to have some quote unquote quality time and all the kids want to do is watch TV, we think we should resign and stay at home.

But how about this: the grass isn't greener on the other side.

The grass is greener where you water it. And the grass that is watered consistently and also fertilized is greenest of all.

Forget those other moms. Or better yet, wish them well. Because for each and every one of us, some days it's the elevator, some days it's the shaft.

Look at your life and deal with the What Is.

Right here, right now.

You're at home with your kids. Good for you. A big part of being a mom is being there. Period. No matter who you are and how you nurture. You're a warm, sentimental snuggling mom, or you're a straightforward, no-nonsense mom, but you're a mom who is there. Your joy and your challenge is that. Being there. With them. All the time. So much so, that you've forgotten who you are, besides being the slave to these tiny tyrants.

This is my life. For now, for these few years when my girls are small, I'm in it. I am the mom, the overseer, and the person on duty. Last fall, while we were on Kaua'i, I got a gig in L.A. and I needed to go for a week. I took Brody with me.

Other times, I've had to go to New York, or abroad, and I put on my warrior/tour guide/secretary/professional organizer hat. I pack up the girls—book their tickets, launder their clothes, match their socks, find their hairbrushes, put together snacks, charge up the electronics, all in addition to getting myself together—and haul them, and their babysitter, who watches them while I'm at work, along with me. Could I leave them all at home? Of course. Do I prefer to take the shit storm on the road? Absolutely.

Bela, at sixteen, has her own life. She comes and goes. But while my other girls are little, they're with me. Of course I realize that I'm absurdly lucky to have such flexibility. But just because I'm lucky that doesn't mean I don't lose it on a regular basis.

Working-in-an-office moms have other issues. You're an attorney, a teacher, a phlebotomist. Every morning you leave and every night you come home, hoping you'll have some time to be with your kids before you have to get up and do it again the next morning. Maybe there's a house-husband whipping up the noodles with butter (served with baby carrots from a bag), or maybe you have a nanny. Or maybe you have to scoop the kids up from daycare before six.

Then, finally, you're home, and the clock is ticking on mother-children time, and it's tough. Kids have their own rhythms. You can't nurture them on demand. On the other hand, you experience the deep satisfaction of providing food, shelter, and clothes—or at least some of those things—for your children. They literally couldn't survive without you. Also, you have an identity out in the world; you're not just Sarah and Michael's mommy. You also get a little downtime at work, hanging out in the break room, bopping downstairs for a latte. The kind of breaks mothers at home never get, unless they're blessed with children who nap.

These are the trade-offs.

I see the word "trade-off" and it seems like such an old-fashioned concept, like a black-and-white TV. Even though we give lip service to knowing that we can't "have it all," I think we secretly believe that we can, and because we don't, we need to change something, quit our job if we have one and stay home with the kids; get a job and put the kids in day care if we don't. That damn grass is always beckoning from the other side of the fence.

Deal with the What Is.

Do the best you can.

Do the best you can do and be honest. If your kids get on your case and say, "You work all the time!" it's just something you have to hear. You can point out that this is life. That people work for a lot of reasons, not the least of which is providing for their children. Point out that you're there for them every night and every weekend.

Perhaps you decide that Wednesday evenings are going to be your night together. Maybe you make an effort to get off work early that day, and have your one-on-one time or your one-on-three time. You do a special mommy-three-kid dinner night. And maybe Sunday you have a crazy kid-centered brunch. Whatever it is. You try to carve out time so that you can make those moments mean something.

I'm all for bringing kids into adult-land. It's all well and good to race home and throw on your sweats and roll around on the floor with the kids, but it's equally as good for them to come into your adult world. Maybe once a month your kid spends the last few hours of your workday with you. You pick her up, or someone drops him off, and you set up a little desk, and they get to see what it's like being you.

Last year Laird was featured on Oprah's Master Class series, and one day Reece decided to watch it. She's adores her father and complains often and loudly about how he spends more time in the ocean than he does with us.

One afternoon after I'd picked the girls up from school, Reece asked if we could stop by the surf barn to see him. On the way, she launched into a rant that shows, if nothing else, the girl has a talent for sermonizing.

"Did you know that not counting sleeping Daddy spends more time with the Ocean than with us? Besides Sunday, but that's if there's no swell. All the time he plans his days around what the Ocean is doing."

I tried not to laugh, but I was amused at her ability and willingness to lay it all out there, a daughter's privilege. Could you imagine if I, as his wife, let loose that kind of diatribe?

Then, from the backseat, comes Brody's little voice: "Yeah, he loves the Ocean more than us!"

I tried to explain to the girls that being in the Ocean was both Daddy's job and what makes Daddy *Daddy*. I said that when you love people, you try and understand what they need, and help get them it. "When you want to go off and play with your friends, Dad doesn't guilt you out about it, does he?" I said. I think I might have even thrown in something about "How do you think we buy toys?"

Reece is no pushover. I could tell she wasn't convinced and was just waiting for me to stop talking. Finally, she said, "I know it's his job, but he likes it too much. Even when he hangs out with me what do we do? He takes me surfing. Where? The Ocean." She was committed.

I think she moved off her position a little when she watched the documentary. I could see by the expression on her face that she had a new appreciation for what her dad did, for what he has done, and for how he views the world.

Don't be afraid of showing your kid what it is you do all day. You can take a kid who's seven or eight to the office, and let her watch you working the phone, or making a decision or arriving at an agreement, having your assistant coming in and out and buzz buzz buzzing. Then, when you tell them at home that you're going to work, they know what that means. They still might not have any real clue what you're doing there, but they know that something happens there. It's not just this mysterious place that takes you away from them.

OBLIGATORY BASEBALL METAPHOR

Often, I think of it like this: rather than running around bemoaning how overwhelmed you are, consider a baseball game. The pitcher and first baseman are working all the time. They're part of the game, part of the outcome, part of the action. They're not just standing in the outfield, twiddling their thumbs. The game is won or lost depending on how they play.

Like them, we are high-impact people. In the office, with our partners, with our children, and in our community, we're always involved. It may be exhausting, but it's much richer and more fulfilling than being out in right field.

DON'T IMPALE YOURSELF

No matter what's going on in your life, whether you're a mom working at home, or a mom working at the office (or a dad working in the ocean), don't punish yourself. Guilt not only accomplishes nothing, it often prevents us from making real changes. A friend who used to write a column for a major magazine noticed over the years that many of the questions she received were from women who lived in a state of perpetual guilt because they didn't think they spent enough time with their kids, or they spent all their time with their kids and secretly hated it, or they worked part-time and when they were at work they felt as if they should be at home and when they were at home they felt as if they should be at work. The one thing they all had in common is that they were clobbered by guilt. But it was as if admitting to feeling guilty, they didn't have to change anything. They were snuggled up in their guilt security blankets.

They were also surprised that their lives were busy and challenging and full of compromises and strife. As if somehow they'd been betrayed by the movie fantasy of being married and a mother that they'd expected. Modern life is complicated, and we're all forced to make choices. To say that you feel terrible about the choice you've made, and then to go ahead with it anyway—that's not a good message to send to your kids. It's putting blood in the water. It's telling them, in essence, that you know you're doing wrong by them.

It's similar to when your child falls down. The other day Brody was taking a nap on the couch and rolled right off and smacked her head on the floor. *Boom!* She rolled over and opened her mouth, but nothing came out. There was a long minute of silence, and then she howled. Laird strode over and scooped her up, but he was matter-of-fact. He checked out the bluish egg already rising on her forehead, trying to evaluate whether or not she was seriously injured. A popular saying will tell you all you need to know about the quality of medical care on Kaua'i: "When in pain, get on the plane."

But he kept telling her she was okay. He didn't panic and say "Oh my god! You hit your head really hard. Are you all right?" Saying that would convey to her that maybe she wasn't all right. (Brody was fine.)

In the end, no matter where we find ourselves, there are lessons to be learned, and the best one might be that life offers no guarantees, and that often you just have to make the best of things. It's no one's fault. It's not as if you could have done anything differently. It's just the What Is.

HOLIDAZED

Sometimes I wonder if what does us in, expectationswise, are the holidays. Would we be able to accept the realities of life behind the white picket fence if we didn't have to stage a never-ending cavalcade of precious-memory-creating holiday celebrations, year in, year out? Especially when it seems as if every year the holiday season is getting longer; these days, it seems as though it starts with Back-to-School (not a genuine holiday, but all that new clothes, backpack and school-supply shopping feels festive) and ends with Easter.

My childhood wasn't easy. After my father died, my mother and I bounced around a lot. So come holiday time, I'm always grateful that I'm not steeped in (imprisoned by) tradition. I don't have to cope, every year, with the feeling that if I don't make my mother's prime rib and Yorkshire pudding on Christmas Eve that I'm not holding up my side of the circle of life. I have a little more familial elbow room around the holidays to do what feels right for the family, right now.

The question should be: Do we serve the holiday, or does the holiday serve us?

It's lovely to have traditions, but one of them should also be the tradition of flexibility. Holidays with infants and toddlers are different from holidays with school-age children, middle schoolers, older teenagers, and college-age kids.

Trying to enforce the same traditions year in, year out is a recipe for depression and heartbreak. We don't force kids to continue to believe in Santa Claus, and neither should we force ourselves to continue to roll out the Hollywood-style Christmas production every year. The year will come when your daughter, who used to love spending a week making snowman cookies with you, has been cast in the winter play at school. Or, she's playing a winter sport. Or, dum-de-dum-dum, she has a boyfriend and wants to spend every waking Christmas-y moment with him.

I realize it's starting to seem as if Laird is the multipurpose go-to man for life lessons, but if you'll indulge me: every morning he wakes up and plans his day according to what the weather is doing, which affects what the ocean is doing.

Every year, take a look around. What's the fall been like? What's going on with everyone? What's going on with *you?* Maybe you've had the flu or been slammed at work or there's been a death in the family. Maybe you're beat. Conversely, maybe you're feeling energized. You got a raise, or a new idea for a business you'd like to start, or your sister who lives in Rome is in town.

Also, there's nothing that says you have to buy your tree the Saturday after Thanksgiving, and have your holiday party the first weekend in December, etc., etc. Some years you might be feelin' it as you plow through those Thanksgiving leftovers and some years it might not hit you until December 15.

These are supposed to be *holidays.* You know, like, joyous. Celebrate accordingly.

I've pinned Christmas on the dartboard here, but you can substitute any holiday.

Thanksgiving is my favorite holiday. I love to have a big meal with a lot of people around the table, say a prayer, and hear what people are thankful for. The occasion is both the holiday and the gift. Perfect.

THE ANTIRESENTMENT DIET

No one forced us to get married and have children. It's the twenty-first century; we can more or less do whatever we want: stay single, or live in a community with a roommate or two. We could simply have lovers, or be one of those women devoted to her agility dogs.

But even if you are someone who gets it, who fully understands that you're going to be working like a merchant marine on a shorthanded ship, putting away every toy in the house at 9:45 p.m., stepping on a doll shoe in your bare feet, which gives you a limp for a week, washing the dinner dishes by hand because the dishwasher is broken and you only remember to call the repairman at three a.m. when you can't sleep because you drank seven cups of coffee during the day. Even if you know all this, and accept it, and embrace it, and even enjoy it most of the time—does anything feel better than pouring yourself a glass of wine and putting up your feet at ten-thirty, after the kids are sound asleep?—the day will come when something happens and you completely, absolutely, and simply lose your shit.·

What causes a total meltdown? Never anything that warrants it. Never anything *reasonable*. Usually it's something that you've said at least five hundred times before. You've said it five hundred times, and the people to whom you've said it—generally the kids, but sometimes the husband—look at you as if whatever it is you're saying is merely contributing to the ambient room noise. It's like you're the TV left on for company, or the sound of rain on the roof, or the air-conditioning switching on. Nothing anyone needs to acknowledge.

When my girls get ready for their day, all I ask is that they brush their hair, brush their teeth, and wash their hands. This is all I insist upon. Hair, teeth, hands.

Reece and Brody are good about their hair, good about their hands, but they aren't very interested in brushing their teeth. They lie to me and say they've brushed, but then I make them come over and I do a breath check and they have bad little kid breath and we go back and forth, endlessly, about whether they did or whether they didn't brush their teeth. Sometimes Reece complies by brushing her teeth for five seconds, just long enough so her breath smells minty.

Then one day, I discovered that Brody was putting a dab of toothpaste on her tongue to give her breath that minty smell.

I. Went. Crazy.

"You went to all that effort of getting out the toothpaste and squirting some on your tongue but you won't brush your teeth! You're already opening the toothpaste! You're already putting it in your mouth! Can't you just brush your teeth! What would it kill you to brush your teeth! You know what? Fine. Fine fine fine. Do I care if your teeth turn black and fall out of your head? No I do not! And when they do, by the way, don't think I'm taking you to the dentist. Don't think I'm doing one thing to prevent you from becoming toothless and sad, never able to bite into another apple as long as you live. And if you think I'm giving you one sweet treat today, you are mistaken. No chocolate, no candy, not even a stick of gum. Not even Pirate's Booty. You get nothing. Why can't you just brush your teeth! How many times do I have to ask you to brush your teeth!"

Everything that comes into my head I say. I stomp around the house like a lunatic.

Reece and Brody just look at me, live reality TV, the part where Crazy Mom Loses Her Mind, right before their very eyes. They watch me and when I demand a response, they shrug and go *t'huh.*

Nothing, of course, has been solved.

It's okay.

This was a tough one for me to absorb. Even though I'm a blond beachy-looking girl, I'm not hang loose. I like to be in control, and since I've had my kids I no longer feel in control, ever. Maybe this was a function of being single and childless, but in my twenties, I felt organized.

But now? What a laugh. When I close my eyes and think of myself on an average day, I imagine a dog chasing her tail in the bed of a truck without brakes on a mountain road. My long life in sports has trained me not to react, outwardly, to stress. I go about my tail-chasing business. Maybe my eyes look a little buggy from the pressure I feel behind them. But some days, without warning, I lose it.

And sometimes it just feels good to let it out.

Not only does it feel good, it's imperative. I'm not suggesting that you bathe in the drama of a situation. I'm not saying that you should belabor the point after you've had a fit. You shouldn't.

But do honor and enjoy your hissy fit. Even if you've acted irrationally, it's never good to eat your rage. Counselors and shrinks generally frown on acting out, but if not acting out is going to result in growing resentment of your situation, then throw a dish. A broken dish can be swept up, and you can apologize. It's much more difficult to eradicate resentment once it's taken hold.

Resentment is the kudzu of the heart. It's black mold and head lice and every other nasty thing that's nearly impossible to get rid of. What's worse, it leads to contempt, and contempt for your life, your partner/husband, even your children (it happens) leads to one thing only: game over. Contempt is defined as feeling something is worthless, or beneath one, and once it has grabbed ahold of you, it's almost impossible to recover from.

So, don't feel guilty or bad for blowing off steam; you really are doing it for the good of yourself, your marriage, and your family.

After I had my meltdown, I calmed myself down by taking a step back and asking myself how I could better deal with things.

It all came down to exercise.

Movement equips you with the ability to gain perspective.

I realized that if I didn't get up first thing in the morning and exercise, it would be more difficult to get things done and maintain my perspective as the day progressed. Some mornings I just get up, throw on my gym clothes, and *go*. A mere thirty minutes is all it takes. (If you're worried that you don't have time, just think of how much time and emotional energy a meltdown consumes.) Jogging is good, but so is walking meditation. Some people talk to God on their morning hustles. Whatever. The point is: exercising and eating well is armor against the chaos that is our lives.

The other thing I did after my freak-out was to make a list of what's important. Everyone has their own list; it really does help to write it down because once it's written you know: everything that's not on the list should be immaterial to you, water off a duck's back. Who cares? Not you.

My list:

1. Be thankful for everything, even the hard stuff.
2. Take care of my health (eat well and exercise).
3. Be the best mom and wife I can for my family.
4. Try to be kind.
5. Work hard and stand up for what I believe.

If things fall under one of those umbrellas, then I'm dead serious. Everything else, I'm going to try to keep it in perspective. And if I blow it, that's cool. The next morning I'll have another opportunity to cope with unnecessary crap, reminding myself that the only time you fail is when you stop trying.

11

BE THE QUEEN

In Kaua'i Laird does his inventing, building, reworking, and noodling around in a barn, but in Malibu his workshop is the garage. Last June he went to France as part of his duties as the spokesman for Oxbow World Surfwear Company. Before leaving for the airport he stood in the driveway with his hands on his hips, stared into the disarray in the garage, and said, "I have to get everything out of here, clean it, and edit it. Everything."

I had what I thought was a brilliant idea. For Father's Day I would clean out the garage, and over the next week, while he was away, I dragged everything out, had the walls and the floor repainted, and ordered new cabinets. His bikes, boards, and tools sat in the driveway beneath a huge blue tarp, await-ing his return. I was proud of this present. We have everything; there's not one more thing on earth that we need. Helping Laird get his workshop in order could not have been a better gift.

Laird came home the day before Father's Day. Oxbow was celebrating its twenty-fifth birthday, and he'd spent the entire week going from meet-and-greet to interview to party and back. The meetings, receptions, appearances, and interviews began at seven a.m. and lasted until midnight. For a guy who spends most of his days either alone tinkering, or out on the ocean with a friend or two, nothing is more exhausting for him than all this face time and interacting with other humans.

The moment I saw him I could tell he was in a Mood. The Weatherman was experiencing a tropical storm of discontent. He had that heavy look he gets, his brow lowered, his mouth a straight line. I had expected him to be wiped out, but I wasn't expecting this. Nevertheless, I pressed on with my plans, stopping at Whole Foods on the way home to pick up a few things. He sat in the passenger seat with his arms folded, scowling. Was I really going to drag him to a busy grocery store?

Yes, yes I was.

The minute we pulled into the driveway and he saw the tarp-covered mound of stuff, the rear wheels of his bikes pok-ing out, he sat bolt upright. "What's all that stuff doing out there?"

"Happy Father's Day!" I said, opening the garage door.

The space was clean and empty, the walls covered with a fresh coat of white paint.

"Now I have to put all this stuff back in," he snapped. "And it's been raining."

"It's under a tarp," I said.

"This is unbelievable. You stuck my stuff out in the rain."

I turned on my heel and walked into the house. I could hear him grumbling to himself outside.

"Well, that went over well," I said to Bela.

"He's probably just tired," she said.

He's probably just an asshole, I thought, but didn't say.

I thought, briefly, of going to a hotel. I wanted to be in a hotel. I imagined the huge empty bed, the solitude, the merciful absence of a big, angry big-wave surfer stomping around and swearing under his breath.

Instead, I went to bed. But the next morning I stayed in bed. This is unlike me. We're an early-to-bed, early-to-rise kind of family. By six-thirty I'm usually in the kitchen whipping up a smoothie. Not today. Today I lay there and remembered how, when he'd seen his girls, he wrapped them up in a big hug, how he'd kissed the tops of their heads. He'd been gone only a week. They were like puppies, all so happy to see one another. I stood there and watched. The wife.

I wondered whether this was the end. Maybe we'd been together too long.

The next day was interesting. Naturally we hadn't had sex in a week, and under other circumstances I'd grab him for a little nap date, but I was livid. We passed each other in the kitchen.

GABRIELLE REECE

"I love you," he said.

"Phooey," I said.

"Can we just forget about the way I behaved yesterday?" he said.

I wound up forgiving him—he really was trashed from his long week and thirteen-hour flight from Paris. It was one of the many times I've tried to manifest the best advice I've ever heard about making marriage work: be short on memory, long on forgiveness.

Losing my marriage to Laird isn't a happy thought. I'd be heartbroken if we divorced, but my human existence wouldn't be threatened. Still, the idea of splitting up doesn't leave me panic-stricken. I never think: I better do whatever it takes to make this work because otherwise I'll be living out of a shopping cart under a bridge. I have enough skills and enough faith in my ability to stand on my own two feet; I'm completely confident I could feed and clothe myself and my kids.

Once, Laird said to me, "If I left tomorrow, your life would barely change."

And I thought, "Isn't it great?"

Laird's love of freedom and spontaneity is legendary. I wouldn't have it any other way; I orchestrate our lives so that Laird can be Laird. Still, there are many nights when I roll over and look at his head on the pillow and think, *You could be gone tomorrow.*

I rarely dwell on the risky nature of Laird's profession—in part because he's always alert and prepared. He doesn't get too comfortable, thinking, *Oh, this is only a fifteen-foot wave, yawn.* He's neither cavalier nor foolhardy. He's truly humbled by the ocean. Still, the day always comes when he gets word there's a swell off the coast of Maui or Tahiti or Indonesia or New Zealand, and he's up before the sun, rushing around in preparation. I can feel the anticipation coming off him in waves.

I'm not much of an astrology girl. When a friend tells me her car keeps breaking down because Mercury is in retrograde, I laugh. But whenever I have a strong feeling about something, I heed it, absolutely. Once, Laird was headed off to Pe'ahi, to the infamous break known as Jaws, so-named because it's as unpredictable and as fatal as a shark attack, and I called him, catching him on his cell minutes before he and his crew set off on their Jet Skis for the deep water. I said, "Keep an eye peeled today, Lover." That day he wiped out, his board came back at him and broke his shoulder.

Living this way, I'm always aware how fragile life is, how precious. And how things can go south at any time. Shit really does happen, as the bumper sticker tells us. Even if the divorce rate weren't holding steady at about forty-eight percent, even if we all mated for life like geese, the reality of human existence is precarious. Anyone of us could get hit by a car, fall off our bikes and split our heads open, contract a fatal disease. I'm not suggesting that we should obsess over it, but to think it will never happen to us is to set ourselves up for a nasty surprise. Of course, we'd prefer not to think about it because it's scary as hell.

And even if you've been blessed and nothing too terrible happens, and your partner is the poster child of consistency and a reliable provider, your children still are going to grow up and leave. And before that they're going to become teenagers who want nothing to do with you. They'll be out of the house at school or hanging with friends, and when they're home they'll be holed up in their rooms with the doors closed. They will allow you to serve them, of course, but do you really want to be one of those moms who scurries around after her fifteen-year-old picking up his dirty socks, "helping" him write his paper on the causes of the Civil War, and chauffeuring him hither and yon, just to prolong your feelings of being indispensable? One of the best things we can do as parents is to teach our kids to be independent; hovering over young adults as if they were in kindergarten is doing them, as well as yourself, a big disservice.

Empty-nest syndrome isn't just a punch line. If you had your children at thirty, by the time you're fifty they're launched, and there you are, wandering around a house with too many bedrooms, grocery shopping for two. If you've been taking care of yourself, and are lucky enough not to have any health issues, you've got another thirty or more years of life ahead of you, roughly the same number of years in which you had no children to raise.

A friend's college-age daughter gives horseback riding lessons and the little seven-year-olds are always amazed that this young woman of twenty is so old. One little girl was completely flabbergasted. "You're three times as old as me!" she cried. "You could have *children.*" How endearing is that, how naive? And yet my thirty- and fortysomething friends with school-age children look at the women they know who have young adults and think their own kids will never be that old. Since they define themselves first and foremost as mothers, they'll never truly figure out, as the poet Mary Oliver so famously said, "what to do with your one wild and precious life."

However devoted we are to our families, and however seriously we take our role as mothers—and I take it very seriously—being a parent isn't our only role, and I don't think it ever pays to take ourselves too seriously. We're moms. There have been millions before us and there will be millions after us. We may be the sun and the moon for our little ones, but we haven't been tasked with destroying the Ring in the Mountain of Doom and saving mankind.

When I drop Reece or Brody off at school or ballet, I don't have to be in full Mommy mode. I'm just Gabrielle, going about her day. And I want my girls to see that there's more to being a woman than just serving her family.

Not long ago, at the end of one of those monstrously long days that began at five a.m. with Brody waking me up for a glass of water, even though the one I'd put on her nightstand at two a.m. was still there, minus a single sip, Reece asked me to name the four happiest days of my life.

Four? I thought, *Four?* I was tired and vaguely irritated. I didn't think I could count that high. It was something of a setup, because Reece already had the answers.

"The day you met Dad!" she said.

Did I roll my eyes? It's possible.

"I know!" she said. "The day you married Dad. The day you met Bela. The day I was born and the day Brody was born."

The inside of my eyelids felt like sandpaper, but I took the opportunity to talk to Reece about how, as happy as those days certainly were, there were also other happy days. I talked to her about self-definition, and the importance of being your own person, no matter where life takes you, no matter whether you marry and have children or not.

I told her about my deep love of volleyball, and how every game, in its way, was a source of happiness whether we won or lost. I told her how it was my ticket out of an uncertain future. Volleyball brought me an education, a job I loved, and, ultimately, led me to her father. I recalled a time when I was playing professionally, when we'd just finished a night tournament in Detroit. We'd won the tournament, in part because of my contributions. The team had been struggling for a while before that win, but we'd come together when it counted. I can still feel the sweat on my back, the weird northern-style humidity of that place, the smells of evergreen trees and fresh water.

Reece was perplexed. She couldn't imagine that there might be something that I, her mother, might do that would make me happy that didn't in some way revolve around her and our family.

OCCUPATIONAL THERAPY

If you're at home in the trenches with the toddlers you're probably not also going to be teaching yourself Arabic or computer coding, or keeping up your litigation skills on the off chance you have to get a job, pronto. But you should be spending some time during an average week doing something for yourself, if only to remind yourself that you have a self that actually enjoys something unrelated to being a wife and mother.

"Enjoyment" comes in a lot of different colors. Me, I like to work hard. Two daughters of two different friends just graduated from eighth grade and want to try out for their high school volleyball teams. I offered to take them to the beach with a bag of balls and train them. One of the girls had trouble with her serves and we stayed at the beach an hour longer than I'd planned, just so I could keep drilling her. I was determined to see some progress, and I wanted her to see some, too. That was fun for me.

You might have a crappy job that's just a job. Many people do, and if you're one of them, you also need an outlet, an occupation, that's for you and you alone. Train for a 10k, bake some badass pies, start a book group and take it seriously (really read and think about the books). I have a friend who's started a small business making gift baskets. It's creative and she makes some extra cash and it gives her a chance to reconnect with a part of herself that she hasn't been able to express in a long time.

And there's something else: being defined as a person helps you cope with the pure terror that comes with having a child. We are so vulnerable. Our hearts are on the line. We've brought a being into this unfair, unpredictable world, in the process creating something the loss of which can break our hearts so thoroughly we will never recover.

That is scary shit.

And by the way, it's part of why we're so tight and intense in our parenting: "Watch your fingers." "Don't stand too close to the edge." "Don't go in the deep end." "Stay away from that dog." "Put down the scissors." "Take that out of your mouth." "No, you can't have a skateboard." "Call me when you get there."

One modest way to help us stay sane is to do things that help us develop and maintain a sense of who we are, apart from our family. You've got to be anchored in yourself. In a lot of ways it's a daily practice.

KEEPING THE GIRL SPIRIT ALIVE

It's one of those old sayings that always comes with a heaping serving of disapproval and a side of eye roll: Boys will be boys. And so will men. To which I say, Thank god.

Maybe it's because that somewhat corny old saying "A man works from sun to sun, but a woman's work is never done" is so accurate it's turned us into humorless multitasking taskmasters.

As you know, I'm all about work, about grinding. I'd be miserable if I didn't have a lot of work. When I go to a hotel and have a single bag, and the bellman asks if he can carry it, I'm completely unable to hand it over. I have to carry it myself. Asking me to invest my time in something silly is like trying to turn a herding dog into a purse dog: misery for everyone concerned.

With all this said, women need to lighten up. All this hyper-domestication is making us resentful, miserable, and if not literally killing us, killing the girl spirit that lives inside us. Many of us scoff about the way guys love girls. We always think it's purely sexual, but I think there's another component: girls are light, playful, and free. They're up for adventure. When we're feeling like a house gnome with a hump on our back and a to-do list as long as our arm, the first thing to disappear from our personality is that sense of lightness and freedom. We become irritable and exacting. We lose our verve.

Everyone's got her own way to keep it alive. I know a few moms who are devoted to their monthly board game night. They have plenty of snacks, gin and tonics, free-range hilarity. It would seem completely pointless. Unless, of course, you happen to believe that the point of life is to have fun.

You remember having fun, don't you? And I don't mean creating a situation is which your children can have fun and you draft off their enjoyment. Chuck E. Cheese can be a blast at a four-year-old's birthday party, but would you ever go there for any reason with someone who had her adult teeth? I don't think so.

Yes, kids are hilarious, and every moment you can enjoy that part of raising them you should. They live to gobble up all your attention, and so they are expert entertainers. It's one of nature's tricks. It keeps us from putting them up for sale or leaving them by the side of the road when they've been screaming for four hours straight. When they're in their best cutup comedian mode, you really do owe it to yourself and to them to laugh your ass off.

But you've got to create some fun for yourself that isn't about your kids. It can be as simple as throwing on your sneakers and go bopping around the lake, with your ponytail swinging behind you. Doesn't matter whether you're twenty-seven or sixty-seven. A forty-year-old ponytail is still a ponytail. When you jog around that lake, take the time to look around, check out your surroundings, take a personal inventory. Liberate yourself. If you can have a few girlfriends along, all the better. Have a laugh whenever you can. What's on your iPod? Hopefully tunes that recall a time when you were open to everything life had on offer, when anything related to schedules or laundry was the furthest thing from your mind.

And cultivating that lightness of spirit isn't just good for you.

Remember, your kids are watching—all the time. And in the blink of an eye they will be grown and trying to figure out life on their own. Don't you want them to be optimistic and joyful, with a sense of life's possibilities? At the very least, don't you want them to think about you with a smile on your face and a bounce in your step, and not someone standing in the doorway of their room with that butt-crack line between your eyes, scowling, telling them to pick up their dirty clothes?

A WORD ON "HAVING IT ALL"

I don't know where this "having it all" business started, but it's fairy-tale bullshit. I'm going to assume that once upon a time "having it all" just meant having the same opportunities as men do. It was an expression of *potential*. Women, whether single, married, or married with children, should have the same options routinely available only to men.

It didn't literally mean having everything. Little children know that life is unfair and that you can't have everything you want. Is that what this inane question means now, in the spoiled rotten times in which we live? Do women really believe they can have and excel at the most perfect and rewarding career, while also experiencing the joy of parenting the exact number and gender of children they desire, living in a perfect home with a happy, hunky husband with whom they have frequent and mind-blowing sex, and also sustain a profound and nourishing spiritual life, while also maintaining the right number of interesting and satisfying friendships, as well as some delightfully distracting hobbies (crafting!), all while being youthful, dewy, tight of ass, firm of upper arm, with an eternally flawless mani-pedi to boot?

Is *that* what people mean? That life is unjust if wanting it all doesn't lead to having it all?

Frankly, I don't know who is having this conversation. Not the twenty-nine percent of co-breadwinning moms, or the nearly forty percent of breadwinning moms, surely. Their version of having it all means being able to take the Friday after Thanksgiving off, being told by the mechanic that the weird knock under the hood isn't the transmission but simply a loose bolt, having a healthy kid without a police record, and being able to spring for a pair of new shoes now and again.

Men don't have it all, and few people seem to fret about that. If a man wants to be a member of a family, he has to figure out how he can be the tough, aggressive guy out in the world, then come home and function as a father with colicky babies and miserable teenagers. He has to go out there every day and slay the mammoth—millions of men have jobs they don't like or find unfulfilling, by the way—then walk back in the door and shift gears and go coach the seven-year-old's T-ball team, then listen to his wife talk about her plans for the kitchen remodel.

Perhaps if I wasn't married to a he-man like Laird, I wouldn't be so aware of this. Being married to him has given me more compassion toward the plight of the male of the species. I think we should cherish our men, have fun, gather, take things less seriously, let things go.

The reality is this: we may think we want it all, we may think we want the so-called happily ever after, but we really don't. Discomfort grounds us and grows us. Why do you think resistance training works? Because it makes your muscles struggle, forces them to become stronger and more efficient.

Not having everything is how it should be. There's no greater catalyst for growth than dissatisfaction. It makes you keep digging that tunnel to your true self, your true life.

But to endure and enjoy the struggle, we need to be the queen, not the princess.

What does it mean to be the queen?

The queen is ageless. She may be a young wife, a new mother, an older mother with many children, a mother whose children are grown and gone.

The queen is kind. The queen is generous. The queen works as hard, if not harder, than everyone else. The queen doesn't sit on the couch saying, "I don't feel like it." The queen is not a victim. She is a cool, nonmanipulative loving partner. She lives by her codes. The queen is the head of the military, she listens to the pleas of commoners, she oversees all of the special celebrations and feast days. She is merciful. And remember, the queen may be fair and the queen may be just, but if you cross her, she *will* cut off your head.

The title is sitting there waiting for you.

And if you choose to take it on?

You will live interestingly ever after.

ACKNOWLEDGMENTS

I share my experiences in this book in an attempt to remind people that happiness is not defined in one way. It's up to each one of us to figure out what it means from moment to moment.

Thank you to Karen Karbo, the smartest, funniest writing partner I could have ever hoped for. I could bounce my ideas off her honestly and safely, and I learned so much from her in the process. Thank you for the honor of collaborating and helping me to have the balls to just say it. You are an amazing friend, and my love and respect for you are boundless.

I would like to tip my hat to everyone struggling to get it done and still figuring out a way to keep a smile on their faces and love in their hearts. Thanks to all of the people who have helped me to figure it out along the way:

My friends, who are bright lights in my life year after year and who are willing to call me on my BS when I need it: Jennifer Meredith Castillo, Becky Pollack Parker, Kelly Meyer, Nancy Truman, Cirene Revan, Alexandra Drane, Caridyn Colburn, Tiffany Spencer, Jessica Hall, Shannon Lickle, Twanna Walker Taylor, Harper Reese, Sara Ell, Hutch Parker, and Cecile Reynaud.

Katie Dawson Roberts for your time and love for my family over the years, and for offering a single woman's perspective on the book.

Susan Casey for taking time to read the book and give me your thoughts and support.

Courteney Cox for your love and support.

Chelsea Handler for a complete hard time.

Don Wildman for your friendship and for being a constant source of inspiration to our family.

Jane Kachmer for helping me to have the vision to turn the blog into a book.

Carol Kachmer for help keeping the Hamilton clan on course. We could not do it without you.

My love to the Reece, Borde, Glynn, and Zuccarello families. You are all a part of me wherever I go.

My wonderful editor, Shannon Welch, for her stellar guidance, and Scribner for taking a chance, giving this book a home, and seeing it through from start to finish.

Todd Cole for creating images that give us a sliver of the

chaos, but making it seem just a little more dialed than the reality.

My beautiful and crazy daughters, Bela, Reece, and Brody Jo. You three are the greatest teachers I may ever know, and I am honored to be able to share life with you.

Last, to my king, Laird. Thank you for your understanding, love, passion, and for giving it your best each day. You have made my life so full of color and excitement, and without you. I may have just played it safe. I cherish the gift of knowing you, your love, and your partnership. Oh, and when our girls are difficult, I do blame you for those traits.